NO B.S. SALES SUCCESS

NO B.S. SALES SUCCESS

Dan Kennedy

Self-Counsel Press Inc.
a subsidiary of
International Self-Counsel Press Ltd.
USA   Canada

Printed in Canada.

First edition: January 1994; Reprinted: July 1994; July 1996
Second edition: May 1999

Cataloging in Publication Data

Kennedy, Dan S., 1954-
No b.s. sales success

(Self-counsel business series)
ISBN 1-55180-230-9

1. Selling. I. Title. II. Series.
HF5438.25.K45   1999   658.85   C99-910318-0

Self-Counsel Press Inc.
a subsidiary of
International Self-Counsel Press Ltd.

1704 N. State Street   1481 Charlotte Road
Bellingham, WA 98225   North Vancouver, BC V7J 1H1
USA   Canada

CONTENTS

INTRODUCTION

HOW CAN YOU STEP UP TO BIG LEAGUE INCOME AND SUCCESS IN SELLING?

I hope you've purchased this book to answer that question for yourself. There are a great many things this book is NOT. It is NOT, for example, a textbook approach to selling. It is not about moral or spiritual philosophy (those matters are left to you). It is not even about the psychology of selling. It is noticeably free of all the trendy new terminology so many sales trainers and authors seem to be fond of. And it is not a motivational book either.

It is, simply, a straightforward, relentlessly pragmatic, "no b.s." presentation of what REALLY works in selling.

Not what should work. Not the academic theories about selling. What REALLY works.

You may not thoroughly enjoy this book. It may make you uncomfortable. Confronting, challenging, and rethinking long-held beliefs and habits is provocative and often profitable, but rarely comfortable or enjoyable.

My aim is very simple: after reading this book, I intend for you to implement behavioral and procedural changes that will immediately and dramatically increase the income you earn from selling. This book is all about putting more money in your pocket, nothing loftier than that, nothing less than that. And if we have to break a few eggs to make that omelet, then that's what we'll do.

BECOMING A MEMBER OF THE ELITE

I think this book has an importance that goes beyond the simple issue of finances. A few examples will explain why.

Everybody thinks everybody else has an easier time of it. As I'm writing this, I'm sitting in the first-class section of a United Airlines flight, foregoing breakfast, and on my way to a meeting with Fran Tarkenton, former NFL superstar turned enormously successful entrepreneur. Many people discount Fran's business achievements; after all, he must have had it easy — as a famous football player, he could get through just about any door and get just about anybody to listen to him.

That much is true. However, he couldn't get them to take him seriously. Fran had to fight the "dumb jock" stereotype at every turn. When he found a computer company he was eager to lend his formidable management skills to, even after establishing a successful management consulting firm, he was unable to get the capital needed from banks or any other source. He had to dip into his own pockets and take a multimillion-dollar risk. He bet on himself, but no one else wanted to.

Fran took a down-and-out computer software business and turned it into a huge, $150-million winner. Today, Knowledgeware is a real force in the custom software business, and Fran has gained respect for his innovative ideas about management, team-building, creativity, and problem solving, from his own employees and from business leaders worldwide.

***

I have a long-time friend and speaking colleague, Lee Milteer, who, in a fairly short time, climbed the ladder from a "journeyman seminar leader" working for a public seminar company for low wages to one of the highest-paid, most sought after people in the speaking business. When I first met her, she was deeply in debt, failing to establish herself in this business. Today, she commands fees in excess of $5,000 a day. After several years as a regular "guest expert" on the number one TV talk show in Canada, she now writes a syndicated newspaper advice column.

Lee happens to be strikingly attractive. When she enters a room, most heads turn. Because of that, some people discount her business and career accomplishments; after all, it's obviously easy for such a beautiful woman to get and command attention. And it's true she has no trouble getting attention. But she has had a lot of trouble being taken seriously.

Lee has lugged the "pretty but dumb blonde" stereotype around with her everywhere she's gone. Many people assume that because she looks like a model she must only be "about" lipstick and shopping. Some assume that whatever success she has comes only as a result of her looks. In spite of hauling around this baggage, Lee has built an extraordinarily successful career in a tough, competitive field.

***

Joan Rivers lost her husband to suicide and her network TV show both in the same year. She found herself alone, unemployed, and in financial trouble. Her agent dropped her, advising her that she was no longer marketable.

She started back by taking the only job she could get: a "permanent guest" spot on "Hollywood Squares" for $800 a week.

Two years later, she won an Emmy for her new talk show and, shortly after that, her relationship with QVC, a jewelry company, made her a multimillionaire. Today, she's an entertainment and business empire in and of herself.

Without knowing the details, people may think that things were easy for Joan Rivers because she is famous. But in fact, her earlier success and fame was a huge burden. Known for her humor about marriage and relationships, she became an "untouchable" to many after her husband's suicide.

Today, Joan is wealthy, successful, and in demand in the entertainment world. She has diversified her entrepreneurial activities, and she is admired by her peers and the public.

***

I could continue telling stories of people who overcame their setbacks and obstacles with sales skill and power. Fran Tarkenton's first big business success came about when he locked himself in a hotel room for a week and wore out the phone, selling his idea. Lee Milteer mischievously invented a fictitious staff person and, impersonating that person, sold "Lee" to clients and to the media in the early years of her career. These people have sharply honed, highly effective sales instincts and skills, and no bashfulness about using them every minute of their existence. They have sold their way to the top.

I find this to be true of just about every notable success, in just about every field. The hidden commonality, the "secret" behind so many successful individuals, is the willingness and ability to *sell.*

That's why I insist, without apology, that this book has importance far beyond that of a how-to text for sales professionals. Certainly the ideas I've assembled here should increase any salesperson's earnings. But to compartmentalize selling only to the career is narrow-minded and shortsighted. Instead, you can use these ideas not only to sell your way to the top of your chosen field, but to sell your way to respect and prestige, to fulfilling relationships, to great confidence, security, and peace of mind.

In the last few years, I've pretty much hit the zenith of my speaking career. I've appeared in many U.S. and Canadian cities on public seminar programs with Zig Ziglar and, occasionally, other famous speakers and celebrities, addressing audiences of 3,000 to 5,000 people — and have been paid over $10,000 per 90-minute appearance. My other available days for speaking and seminar engagements are bought by corporate and association clients well in advance. My calendar is full; I say no to many. My lowest per-day fee is $3,850.

Audiences literally stampede to the back of the room to invest their own hard-earned dollars in my books, cassettes, and how-to systems. My own seminars fill rapidly, and entrepreneurs travel from all over the world and pay $3,495 per person to get into my three-day marketing seminars. My total income from speaking rivalled that of the top 2% of the entire profession last year, including very talented people in this business who have been at it for at least a decade longer than I, and including people for whom speaking is their only full-time activity. (For me, it is a part-time enterprise.)

It might surprise some people to know that for several years I stuttered almost uncontrollably. I still stutter occasionally today, usually if I'm very tired or under stress. I still wonder if I'm going to get "hung up" on a word and embarrass myself every time I step up on stage and take the microphone. It might also surprise some people to know that the only time I've spent at a college has been to visit my first wife at her office, watch a football game, or speak to Herb True's classes at Notre Dame.

I have no formal training of any kind relevant to public speaking. I violate most of the rules about how it's supposed to be done, and most of my peers in the profession have never taken me seriously. In spite of more than ten years in speaking, never earning less than a six-figure income, with over 70% of all my engagements breeding repeat engagements, I've only once been invited to speak at the convention held by the professional association I belong to (years ago, in a small break-out session workshop). I've yet to get a speaking bureau interested in representing me.

But none of that has kept me from selling my way to the top. You see, when you determine that you will sell your way through life and sell your way to your aspirations, then you no longer need to wait around for someone to discover you, notice you, accredit you, promote you, or take you seriously. All the power moves from them to you.

You also gain a very special kind of personal confidence and self-assurance. I know that you can drop me out of an airplane into any city with nothing but the clothes on my back, $100 in my pocket, and my sales ability and I'd have a good job and a place to live in 24 hours. Literally millions of people live in constant worry over losing their jobs, their homes, their meager savings. I have no such anxiety and never will. Not that I'm eager for tragedy; I'm certainly not. As comedienne Totie Fields said, "I've been rich and I've been poor, and rich is definitely better." But I do NOT live in fear of loss either.

Mastering the strategies and techniques described in this book can free you from the worries, fears, anxieties, and insecurities suffered by the vast majority of the people around you, from pauper to prince. You join a rather elite, different group with these skills.

I invite you into that group. The welcome mat is out.

ABOUT THE STRUCTURE OF THIS BOOK

This book is divided into five parts. In Part 1, I describe the 16 strategies that I use most in selling. Each is a stand-alone application and any one of them alone could significantly improve your results in selling. But they can also be linked together differently for different situations for increased value and power.

In Part 2, I deal with what goes on before selling can even begin: finding, attracting, and getting into a selling situation with a prospect. As you'll see, I'm no fan of the way most salespeople out carry this job. Here you'll discover some rather radical ideas.

In Part 3, I provide a framework for selling. The various pieces described in Parts 1 and 2 can be plugged in and out of this structure.

In Part 4, I reveal my personal, best, most valued, contrary approach to selling. It may not be for everybody; it may not be for you. Frankly, I argued with myself about putting it in or leaving it out. I ultimately decided I would not be playing fair with you if I sold you a book about selling and held back the information most responsible for my own success. Use it as you will, and good luck.

In the last decade, the sales world has been flooded with new technology, and Part 5 of this edition contains a bonus update section on my "no b.s." observations of this.

PART 1

SIXTEEN NO B.S. STRATEGIES FOR EXCEPTIONAL SUCCESS IN SALES, PERSUASION, AND NEGOTIATIONS

1
STRATEGY #1:
IGNORING THE WORD "NO"

My first sales position (and the only time I've been employed by someone else) was a wonderful training ground. I learned a lot from my experiences in that position, and you'll notice throughout this book that I refer to it a number of times.

I was hired as the central states sales representative for a Los Angeles–based book publisher. I was assigned Ohio, Kentucky, Indiana, Michigan, and Pennsylvania. My job was to call on all the bookstores, department store book departments, discount stores, gift shops, and other retailers in that territory to service existing accounts and open new ones. Most of the company's books were humorous, impulse-purchase items. In many stores, the line of books was merchandised on the publisher's six-foot-high spinner racks, which I had to inventory and stock.

One minor fact that was not discussed when I was hired was that my territory had been "orphaned," and the established accounts had received no service of any kind for eight months or longer. I soon discovered that some of the accounts were a trifle annoyed at having been sold this line of merchandise, promised service, and then ignored.

I was furnished with a computer printout of all the accounts and their purchase history. The first one I visited, a drugstore, provided a clue that things might not be well. I walked up to the owner, introduced myself as the new representative from the company, and watched a mild-mannered pharmacist turn into a raving lunatic. He grabbed me by the arm and dragged me into the back room where he showed me a pile of rack parts that had been shipped in, but that he had been unable to assemble. Surrounding that mess was a stack of boxes full of books. He told me that he had been invoiced for books and racks and had been dunned by a collector for payment, even though he had never had a chance to get the books on the floor to sell. He literally threw the rack parts out of the back door while screaming at me to take it all away.

In the next few weeks, I met with similar antagonism at almost every account I called on. I took a lot of racks and a lot of inventory out of stores. Besides being generally unpleasant and occasionally hazardous to my health, this situation was an economic disaster. I was being rated as a sales rep, and my bonuses were based on a "positive sales ratio" for the month. That means: sales less returns equals net sales.

The way I was going, I would have a negative sales figure for my first month — maybe my first year. I determined that something had to change, and I had to be the one to create the change.

That decision alone is an important tip about getting your own way. It doesn't much matter whether we're talking about selling, like the work I was doing, or negotiating business deals, or running a business. Anybody can look good and get good results when everybody else is cooperating and everything is going as it is supposed to. Under those conditions, just about anybody can have a good time and make a lot of money.

This often happens in business. When times are good, the CEO looks like a genius and the sales reps look like superstars. But when the first rough waters come along, these same people suddenly look like bumbling idiots. Have they actually changed that much? No — they were never very sharp in the first place.

I made up my mind that I had to sell these angry, neglected customers on keeping our line in their stores and even buying more. I had to get positive results under these very negative circumstances. I had to face customers who had been lied to, inconvenienced, billed for merchandise they couldn't sell, dunned for payment, and otherwise abused, and somehow get them to "forgive and forget." In order to do this, *I had to take my ego out of the way.*

Since I've been involved in training salespeople and working with sales executives struggling to get productivity from salespeople, I've discovered that the number one reason for failure in selling is ego. The person with an inflated ego or with very fragile self-esteem (the two are connected) *perceives refusal as rejection.* When someone says no to such a person, he or she takes it personally.

But confusing refusal with rejection makes selling painful, because more people say no than ever say yes. In my situation, customers were calling me vile names, threatening me, even throwing things at me. I had to remember that it really had nothing to do with me. These people weren't mad at me; they were mad at the previous rep, at the company, or at the situation — but not at me.

I've since learned that just about any time an individual disagrees with me, fails to accept an offer I present, says no to me, or otherwise interferes with my access to what I want, it very rarely has anything to do with me as a person. And since it isn't personal, it doesn't warrant any kind of an emotional reaction. Having control over your emotions gives you a very powerful advantage in selling.

As I approached these hostile customers, I took my emotions out of the situation. No matter what they said, I interpreted it as reasonable, justifiable anger at other people and at a negative situation. I listened. I was patient. I was concerned. And I never got angry. I never got defensive. Finally, when the customer had vented and had nothing more to say, I asked for permission to respond. I stated the obvious: I had no control over the past. I could only exercise control over the present. My job now was to make handling the merchandise so profitable and pleasurable for the merchant that it made up for all the past problems and justified a renewed relationship. Then I shifted right into selling — just as if the customer was new and had never heard of the company, the books, or me.

It worked. But even while it was working, many of the customers questioned my integrity. They wanted to know whether or not I was telling the truth. They asked whether I would keep my promises concerning service. They were skeptical and suspicious. If I had wanted to be thin-skinned, I could have gotten angry with them. How dare they question *my* honesty?

Again, I had to understand that this, too, was nothing personal. I chose to work for a company that had "done them wrong" once. I had to accept the consequences, including guilt by association. Again, I had to set my ego aside.

With this approach, I saved twice as many accounts as I lost. I even returned to that first drugstore and got the merchandise back in. I had discovered that initial refusal, even antagonism, was not necessarily the ultimate result. I discovered that I could change a no to a yes more often than not.

My favorite illustration of all this comes from my first call on the head buyer for the book departments of a major

14

department store chain. I went with one of the company's experienced salespeople, as an apprentice, to watch and learn. I was to carry the samples and keep my mouth shut.

Keeping quiet was no problem; I sat in stunned silence as the other sales rep presented the buyer with one new title after another. As he looked at each book, the buyer kept saying: "This is crap. Do you know that? Why should I have this crap in my store? How can you show me this crap?" The buyer went on and on like that, and *the sales rep did not say a word!* Finally, the buyer picked up one sample after the other and barked: "Ship me ten dozen" or "Ship me 50." This went on for nearly an hour and the sales rep rarely spoke. The buyer criticized and cussed each sample, then ordered. When it was over, the rep had written an order for close to $10,000 — a very, very big order in that business. He and the buyer shook hands, exchanged pleasantries, and we left. I couldn't believe what I had witnessed.

The sales rep said, "You know, he always does that. The first few times I went in there, years ago, I got mad at him. I got defensive. I argued with him. Finally he took pity on me. He asked me a great question: "What do you care what I think of this stuff or say about this stuff as long as I buy a lot of it and my stores sell a lot of it and you make a lot of money?"

For the past few years, I've had the great privilege of touring North America, appearing as a speaker on the same seminar programs with Zig Ziglar, addressing audiences of thousands in each city. Zig Ziglar, a master at closing sales, tells the marvelous story of the saleswoman who couldn't hear a no shouted in her ear, but could hear a whispered yes from 50 paces. That is the right approach: simply ignore the word no.

People start out by saying no to things for many, many reasons. It's sort of an automatic, knee-jerk, defense mechanism. They may not fully understand the matter you are dealing with, and be too embarrassed to admit it. They may not know

15

how to intelligently make a decision. They may lack self-confidence and self-esteem. They may be afraid. They may have financial problems that (in their minds) preclude them from going along with you. There are probably hundreds of possible reasons for "the erroneous no." Don't let it stop you.

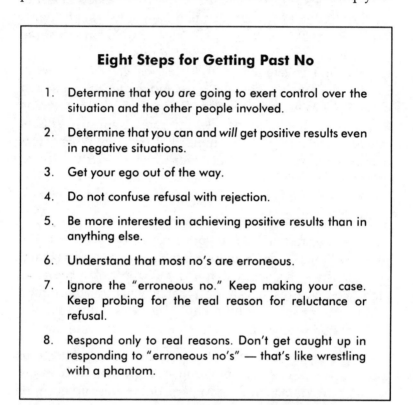

Eight Steps for Getting Past No

1. Determine that you *are* going to exert control over the situation and the other people involved.

2. Determine that you can and *will* get positive results even in negative situations.

3. Get your ego out of the way.

4. Do not confuse refusal with rejection.

5. Be more interested in achieving positive results than in anything else.

6. Understand that most no's are erroneous.

7. Ignore the "erroneous no." Keep making your case. Keep probing for the real reason for reluctance or refusal.

8. Respond only to real reasons. Don't get caught up in responding to "erroneous no's" — that's like wrestling with a phantom.

Understanding, remembering, and using these eight steps will help you convert many initial refusals to ultimate acceptance!

2

STRATEGY #2:
THE POSITIVE POWER OF
NEGATIVE PREPARATION

I've been involved in what I've labeled "the success education business" since 1976. Since 1978, I've been an active member of the National Speakers Association — fraternizing and consulting with hundreds of people who earn their livings as professional lecturers and seminar leaders, including some whose names you know. During that time, I've spoken to nearly 1,000,000 people from the platform, maybe more, about success-oriented topics. I've delivered at least 70 speaking presentations a year, every year from 1978 to 1991, and only in the last couple of years have I deliberately cut back that pace.

As a result, I've had more conversations than I care to count with my students, clients, customers, peers, and friends about "positive thinking." Through it all, I've come to the conclusion that *at least 95% of the people who think they're positive thinkers actually have no idea what positive thinking is really all about.*

Too many people think it's some kind of mystical, magical shield from the real world. They believe that if they just think positive, bad things cannot happen to them. If something bad happens to somebody, they say: "See, you weren't thinking positively." But it just doesn't work that way. You can think positive until you are turning blue from the effort, but you'll still run into obstacles from time to time. People who believe

17

that positive thinking is supposed to keep the bogeyman away eventually wind up frustrated, discouraged critics of positive thinking.

Being a positive thinker does *not* mean that you should refuse to acknowledge the way things are. In fact, people succeed in business, sales, and marketing by dealing with "what is," not with "what ought to be." **The true positive thinker acknowledges potential and existing negative circumstances and reactions, and engineers a plan to overcome them, to achieve positive results.** In selling or negotiating, I call this the positive power of negative preparation.

HOW GENERAL PATTON USED THE POSITIVE POWER OF NEGATIVE PREPARATION

There's a great sequence in the movie *Patton* where General Patton is dozing the night before a battle. He has a book in his lap: Field Marshal Rommel's book on tactics. The next day Patton's troops drive Rommel's troops off the battlefield into retreat. As the gunfire and other noise ends, Patton is standing alone, leaning forward, stage whispering across the battlefield: "Rommel — I read your book."

Some people would say that acknowledging Rommel's expertise as a tactician and preparing to counter any possible successful moves was being negative. They're wrong. It was positively brilliant.

In several of the most successful, profitable, complex negotiations I've been involved in — buying and selling businesses, assembling capital, developing relationships with celebrities, manufacturers, and producers in the TV infomercial business — I've prepared by anticipating and writing down every possible question, concern, and objection the other party could raise, and then formulating my responses in advance. I carefully analyzed every weakness in my position that might be attacked and thought of ways to respond effectively. I thought of every possible thing that could screw up the deal and then thought of some preventive measure to take in each case. I was thoroughly prepared, from a negative perspective.

Another one of my speaking colleagues, the famous motivational speaker Charlie "Tremendous" Jones, says: "You have to plan on your plan going sour so that you have another plan — that's got to be the plan!"

WHO ELSE USES THE POSITIVE POWER OF NEGATIVE PREPARATION?

I have several friends and colleagues in the world of sports. Brendan Suhr, who has been an assistant head coach of the three NBA teams, is one. Another is Bill Foster, former head basketball coach at Northwestern University and one of the "winningest" coaches in college basketball. These guys have super-strength positive attitudes, but they also use the positive power of negative preparation.

Most successful coaches go into each game with more than one prepared game plan. They have a plan to follow if their team gets ahead early in the game. They have a different plan to follow if their team falls behind. They have alternate plans ready to use different combinations of players in case one key player is injured during the game. That's not negative thinking; that's the positive power of negative preparation at work!

I've done a lot of work in planning, scripting, and implementing group sales presentations, and training others to do the same. What I call "group presentation marketing" applies to everything from a Tupperware party to a seminar designed to sell $50,000 real estate partnerships. There are a lot of special techniques for this type of marketing, but one of the most important is the anticipation and removal of the reasons for refusal or procrastination on the audience's part. Sometimes this is done with subtlety, weaving the objections and responses into the presentation. Other times it's done quite openly. One very successful presentation I designed ended with the presenter listing on the blackboard the four main reasons why people don't join — and then answering every one of them. But in every case, every possible problem was thought out in advance and countered somehow during the presentation.

You also have to do this when you are selling in print. When I'm creating an advertisement, brochure, or direct-mail piece, I make a list of every reason I can think of why the reader would *not* respond to the offer. I use that list of "negatives" as a guide in writing the copy. And the other top direct-response copywriters I know, like Gary Halbert, carefully consider these potential obstacles to the sale when crafting a message, too. This approach produces some of the most powerful selling techniques in print in the world.

Six Steps for Using the Positive Power of Negative Preparation

1. Forget preconceived labels of "positive" or "negative."

2. Make a list of every question, concern, or objection that the other person could possibly come up with.

3. Make a list of everything that could go wrong.

4. Develop positive responses to all the negatives you've thought of.

5. Have your information, ideas, and documentation well organized so that you can lay your hands on the appropriate notes and materials at a moment's notice.

6. Take great confidence from your thorough preparation.

3
STRATEGY #3:
USE LISTENING TO INFLUENCE PEOPLE

Here's my super-powerful secret technique: I listen.

Listening isn't as simple as it sounds. In fact, the absence of good listening skills is rated as one of the top problems in North American business today. Some major corporations invest huge sums of money in listening-skills training for their personnel. My biggest complaint with people I work with is their lack of listening effectiveness; I explain something deliberately and precisely, but they get only part of what I'm saying. So, the first problem is that most people lack know-how in listening.

The second problem is even those who CAN listen often DON'T, for all the following and many other reasons:

(a) *They are preoccupied with other thoughts.* If you could see what was going on in the other person's mind, like images on a TV screen, you'd be shocked. Something related to what you are saying might appear every once in a while, but there'd be a rush of other, unrelated images in between. When I'm speaking to an audience, I know that a fast-paced parade of images is going through their heads: a kitchen on fire — "Gee, I wonder if I turned off the coffee pot?"; the supermarket — "What should I make for dinner?"; an angry spouse slamming the door — "She's so unreasonable";

and on and on. They leave me and my presentation, mentally, then come back, leave again, and come back.

(b) *They are tired.* I'm guilty of this one myself. After a few days of traveling, speaking, and consulting, a level of fatigue sets in that just about ruins my ability to listen.

It's worth noting that being properly rested and alert is an advantage in selling or negotiating. The sales pro who stays up too late night after night, or who schedules important meetings too close together, or employs an excessively exhausting travel schedule starts each selling situation with a handicap. Personally, I find both travel and selling activity require incredible physical energy. Avoiding fatigue-inducing foods, sticking to a low-fat diet as best I can, seeing my chiropractor and massage therapist regularly, and taking carefully selected nutritional supplements are all lifestyle techniques I believe give me an edge in my selling activities.

(c) *They are in too much of a hurry.* I recently bought a laptop computer to accompany me on my travels. Writing on paper and sending material by courier home to be retyped was just too slow. I need to have it already typed and printed so I can send it by fax or modem and then download it. When I bought my computer, I had to choose between three models. What was the difference? One was faster than the other, and the third was faster than the second. Speed is the name of the game as we enter the new millennium.

The trick is to use speed to your advantage and to prevent it from becoming a disadvantage. If you have a tendency, as I do, to get caught up in the pace of things going on around you, and to build up stress in the process, it's important to consciously s-l-o-w y-o-u-r-s-e-l-f d-o-w-n in most selling situations. Listening effectively cannot be done at warp speed.

(d) *They are unable to focus their attention.* Many adults today have very poor attention spans. TV advertisers are well aware of this and the need to bring commercials up to "MTV speed" was a topic of hot discussion in the advertising business when I wrote the first edition of this book. You started to see this reflected in TV commercials like the Air Jordan spot with Michael Jordan and Bugs Bunny saving the planet, which premiered during the 1992 Super Bowl, or the "I love this place" Burger King spots. Today, "MTV speed" is the advertising norm. In the infomercial business a couple of years ago, it was the norm to mimic the "Tonight Show"–style talk show and to use what's known in the business as "talking heads." These days you see many more dramatic demonstrations, out-of-studio settings, audience involvement, and similar techniques as infomercial producers fight to hold the attention of the viewer.

As a result of all this, nobody's listening to anybody. And since people generally want most what they have the least of, many are running around in desperate search of someone — anyone — who will make them feel important by listening to what they have to say. There is enormous opportunity in knowing and understanding that.

By training and disciplining myself to listen — really listen — I've been able to exert tremendous influence over many other people. I've gained their trust, stimulated friendship, gotten them to confide in me, and sold to them with ease. I've discovered that you can exchange attention for dollars! I'm now convinced that the person who gets his or her own way most often is the person doing a lot more listening than talking.

HOW TO READ ANYONE'S MIND

Recently, I was summoned to the office of the CEO of a large, fast-growing public company. I was being considered for a very important, very big, very lucrative consulting assignment, potentially worth hundreds of thousands of dollars to me. In the 40 minutes or so of this meeting, we actually dealt with the matter at hand for only ten minutes, and I listened for half of those minutes. For the other half hour, I mostly listened to the CEO talk about his problems of the day, expound on his business philosophy, brag about his most recent big deal, and unintentionally tell me exactly what he wanted to hear from me to make our deal. I sat there and quietly "read his mind."

Dan Kennedy's Truth About Selling #2
You don't have to be a psychic to read
someone's mind — he or she will read it out
loud to you, with a little encouragement!

Five Steps to Listening More Effectively

1. Clear your mind of distractions before getting into a meeting with another person or other people. Take a minute to close your eyes and blank your mind immediately before going into a meeting or picking up the telephone. Top telemarketing trainers tell people handling incoming calls to set aside their paperwork on the first ring, close their eyes and take a deep breath on the second ring, then smile and answer on the third ring.

2. Determine in advance why the person you are going to be listening to is important to you, and why what he or she is saying might be important to you. You have to sell yourself on the relevance in order to focus your attention.

3. Listen for information and insight that you can use to engineer cooperation with the other person. A long, apparently irrelevant, favorite story told by the other person may inadvertently reveal one tiny clue to effectively persuading or motivating that person.

4. Be an active listener. Nod. Give feedback. Ask questions to encourage the person to continue and to demonstrate your interest. Use the technique of "mirroring" to put the other person at ease. This is not to advise sacrificing personality and individuality. I certainly haven't, and I don't believe anybody else should. But you can keep your individuality and still modify your physiology, within a range, to make the person you are listening to feel more comfortable.*

5. In some business situations, it may be appropriate to jot down notes as you listen. Don't hesitate to do so; it helps illustrate your interest.

---

* If you want more information on mirroring, I urge you to read Tony Robbins' book *Unlimited Power,* published by Simon and Schuster.

4

STRATEGY #4:
AVOID CONTAMINATION

In just about every sales organization, there are "grizzled veterans" who, through a combination of longevity, seniority, and accumulated customers or clients, manage to earn reasonably good livings even though they are poor salespeople. These hangers-on make money in spite of their many bad habits. *These people are extremely dangerous to the fresh, enthusiastic salesperson* for a number of reasons:

- They are not fully aware of all their own counterproductive attitudes and habits, and they are capable of unintentionally contaminating others.

- They resent hotshots who might make them look lazy, ineffective, or over-the-hill and will consciously and subconsciously do things to put the hotshot in his or her place.

- They do not keep up-to-date and informed on the latest sales techniques and product information, so they are likely to be sources of outdated or inaccurate information even though they sound authoritative and knowledgeable.

- They often have very poor personal habits, including drinking at lunch and after work on a daily basis, using foul language, and sometimes even poor personal hygiene.

- They are cynical about people. They often call customers or clients "marks," "pigeons," and other derogatory names. *You cannot succeed in selling in a big way if you are cynical about people or about your clientele.* (Note that it's okay to be realistic, just not cynical; there is a difference.)

- They are complainers and blamers — that's how they excuse their own mediocrity. In order to succeed in selling, you must take full responsibility for every factor in the process.

Every business, every company, every organization has at least a few of these types. You will find them on the showroom floor at the car dealership, gathered around the coffee machine in the real estate office, in the hall, or at the sales meeting. You must not let these people contaminate you! You must not let them poison your well!

HOW TO CHEAT ON YOUR EXPENSE ACCOUNT AND OTHER "LESSONS" FROM THE GRIZZLED OLD PRO

Early in my selling career, a manager flew in to work with me in my territory. He and I traveled together for a week. He taught me several creative ways to cheat on my expense account and how to make sales calls by phone and write them up as if they were made in person. He taught me virtually nothing about selling. He was a great "pal." He had a terrific if slightly bizarre sense of humor, and he was making reasonably good money. But he had nothing to offer that would help me achieve my goals.

Shortly after being hired, I went to Chicago to work the company's exhibit booth in the Chicago Gift Show. This is a huge trade show, where tens of thousands of gift shop owners and chain store buyers come in search of new, different, and sellable merchandise. I was excited about being there and eager to write a lot of business with the people attending from my territory. Almost instantly the other sales pros ganged up on me, saying things like, "Take it easy — we're gonna be here for four long days"; "Don't be too aggressive — it looks bad"; "Most of these people are just lookers, not buyers, anyway"; "Nobody sells much at these shows — we're here to get leads."

I ignored the whole bunch of them and, much to their irritation, wrote thousands of dollars of orders during the show. No huge amount — nothing to write home about — but it was more than what five of the others (who had at least six years' more experience than I did) made.

Those experiences taught me that it was generally unwise to listen to advice, complaints, and comments of others just because they were older or more experienced. Age is not necessarily equivalent to wisdom. Experience does not always teach much. In fact, since most people stop learning very early in their careers, you are very likely to encounter the person who has one year's experience 30 times rather than 30 years of experience.

Dan Kennedy's Truth About Selling #3
It's a good idea to learn from other people's experience, but usually with this caveat: seek out and learn from those with experience who are at the top of their game.

You must exercise great care in selecting those who are permitted to advise and influence you. Falling under the influence of someone headed nowhere will generally lead you to the same destination!

There is probably no profession other than selling where mental attitude is as important. W. Clement Stone, self-made multimillionaire, who began as a star insurance sales pro and taught tens of thousands of others how to excel in that field, sums it up this way: "The sale is contingent on the attitude of the salesperson, not the prospect." It is for that reason that you must militantly protect your mental attitude from contamination. Your success will be contingent on your mental attitude, not the attitude of your customers or clients.

5
STRATEGY #5:
THE PROCESS OF
PROFESSIONAL PACKAGING

I have a lot of experience in the advertising business, so I often think in terms of advertising. One big factor in the advertising and marketing of most products is *packaging*. Different packaging is appropriate for different products. Sometimes different packaging for the same product works better in different geographic areas. There are many variables to consider. I think these same considerations apply to packaging yourself.

Like everybody else, I have strong personal preferences about clothing and fashion. I like certain things; I dislike other things. I'm sure you do, too. However, *the successful sales pro learns to set aside his or her preferences in favor of the most effective and appropriate personal packaging for a given situation.* You might think of this as image management. It is critically important.

A prime consideration when packaging yourself is the first impression you give others. Psychologists tell us that most people form impressions of others in the first four minutes of meeting them and that 80% of the impression is based on nonverbal input. What you say has very little to do with it. We also know that people are very reluctant to change their first impressions.

Another consideration is the overall, continuing impression you communicate. You need to always be thinking about what your appearance says about you.

A VALUABLE LESSON FROM
A PREJUDICED BANKER

Early in the operation of my first business — an ad agency — my Monday mail brought back a client's check for a sizable amount marked NSF. (That means "nonsufficient funds," although I'm told that in the South it means "not so fast!") This was not good news. So I jumped in my car and took my client's bad check to the bank, hoping there might be some money passing through that I could intercept. I sat down across the desk from the bank's vice president, passed him his customer's bad check, and told him my story.

The banker said, "As I'm sure you can appreciate, this is the type of matter we prefer to discuss only with the principals of the firms involved."

I handed him my business card and said, "I'm president of the agency. I'm the principal. Let's talk."

He said, in a sincerely surprised voice, "You *can't* be president; you're not wearing a tie."

Of course, I stomped and growled and slammed angrily out of the bank. But later, when I calmed down, I dealt with several interesting issues about success:

(a) *For every one person who says it, there are somewhere between 10 and 10,000 who think it.* All marketing research is based on that premise, and I believe it is sound. Most people are too intimidated or too lazy to express their opinions. Some are only subconsciously affected by something and couldn't enunciate their opinion even though their buying behavior is affected. Most companies count each customer complaint about a given product at 20 or 30 to 1, based on this premise. So the banker's notion about business leaders and neckties has much greater significance than just one solitary opinion from a banker with unfair preconceptions.

31

I do not like this fact, by the way. I wish image wasn't as important as it is. But fooling myself that way wouldn't be very smart. Comforting, but not smart. Comfortable, but not smart.

(b) *In selling, we succeed based on what is, not on what ought to be.* I agree that books should not be judged by their covers. People should not be judged by the clothes they wear or the length of their hair. I argued that point vehemently when my hair was long. But I also know that the reality is that people *do* judge books and people by their covers.

I was at a social gathering this year and listened as the host's daughter, a recent high school graduate, complained bitterly to another guest, a doctor, about her experiences in the job market. She was dressed in a manner that can best be described as a cross between a hippie and a homeless person. The doctor asked if she had gone out seeking employment dressed that way.

"Of course!" she replied. In fact, she had gone to apply for a job behind the counter at a TCBY yogurt shop — where she would be greeting customers and serving food to them — and been told that she could not work there looking like that. "How dare they try to tell me how I can dress?" she demanded, outraged at the injustice of the world.

Sadly, she is not alone in her stupidity.

(c) *Would you rather be right or rich?* I chose the latter, and I've learned to package myself as appropriately and effectively as possible for various situations — to fit the costume to the role. I assure you that it does make a difference.

In my speaking activities, I've experimented and satisfied myself that I sell my educational materials to a higher percentage of an audience when I'm wearing a suit than when I'm wearing a sports coat and slacks. Also, there are clothes I might wear in California that I will not wear in Massachusetts, for example. I've learned these things make a dollars-and-cents difference in my results.

There is no doubt in my mind that the clothes and accessories you wear, the briefcase you carry, the pen you write with, and the car you drive all combine to communicate a message to others that can help you or hurt you. To deny it, to resist it, or to ignore it is self-destructive.

Dan Kennedy's Truth About Selling #4
The logic is simple: if the packaging of products has an impact on how people regard those products, then the packaging of people must have an impact on how others regard those people.

I'm not suggesting that you religiously adhere to everything as if it came from Moses chiseled in rock, but I do suggest you read and carefully consider the information given in John Molloy's *Dress for Success* books.

People prefer dealing with successful people. I want my insurance agent, my real estate agent, my accountant, my lawyer, my doctor, and my public relations consultant to be doing well. The fact that they appear to be doing well indicates that many others agree with my choice and my judgment.

I've also observed that I'm treated with greater courtesy and respect by merchants, store clerks, waiters and waitresses, bank tellers, airline employees, and hotel clerks when I'm dressed for business than when I'm in casual clothes.

Image is part of selling your way through life!

6

STRATEGY #6:
REMEMBERING WHY
YOU'RE THERE

One of the very first speaking engagements I ever had was for a client company at the opposite end of the country from my home. My compensation for speaking was to come solely from the sales of my books and cassettes to the audience; there was no fee being paid. Well, I went and spoke and I was a hit! The audience laughed uproariously, applauded enthusiastically, even gave me a standing ovation at the end! I was back on the plane, halfway home, having a celebratory drink when it dawned on me that I had completely forgotten about the books and tapes hidden under the podium. I had forgotten to give my commercial, forgotten to sell anything, even forgotten to bring the product back with me. *I had forgotten why I was there!*

When Napoleon Hill wrote about "definiteness of purpose," he was surely aiming his remarks at those of us involved in sales and marketing. *Clarity of purpose* is very valuable and very important in advertising, selling, negotiation, and communication. You have to have a clear, single objective.

Many professional salespeople resist this idea and, as a result, never rise above mediocre performance levels. They argue that they have to be concerned with creating and sustaining goodwill, building rapport, developing a friendly relationship, gathering information, and a myriad of other things in addition to selling. Unfortunately, they use these other things as excuses for nonperformance, as camouflage for a real problem — such as the fear of asking for the order. Some salespeople muddle along as "professional visitors."

Dan Kennedy's Truth About Selling #5
A top performer in selling is always focused on selling. He or she takes this attitude, described by Zig Ziglar: you've got my money in your pocket and I've got your product in my briefcase, and I ain't leaving until we make the exchange.

One of the people I made a point of studying, to bolster my persuasive skills in general and my ability to sell to groups from the platform in specific, was Glenn W. Turner, the very controversial founder of Koscot, a cosmetics company, and Dare To Be Great, a self-improvement training company. The two companies together attracted an estimated 500,000 people in just three years to pyramid selling operations — largely through his remarkably powerful speeches. At the time, Glenn Turner was an international phenomenon, receiving immense media attention.

Glenn Turner, by the way, has a speech impediment. He was then and still is pretty difficult to listen to. In his early days in selling, he even had trouble getting hired for straight commission to sell sewing machines door-to-door. Certainly, nobody would pick him as one of the most persuasive public speakers and salespeople of all time.

But there's a film of an old speech by Turner called "Challenge to America," in which he is speaking to an audience of distributors and prospective distributors for one of his companies. He looks right at them and at the camera and says: "It's a good thing I don't have ahold of you cause I'd reach in and extract that check right out of your pocket."

I often think about that piece of film as I enter a "get the check" situation. Is that too tough for you? Is that high pressure? That's the way you've got to be to get what you want.

If you worry too much about peripheral issues — such as being liked, loved, or even respected — or if you "buy into" the other person's problems too much, you'll have a lot of "friends" but not much money.

That's why I think that you've got to take the "hot," new sales training programs with a big, fat grain of salt. There are a lot of different approaches being promoted these days. There's nonmanipulative selling, nonconfrontational selling, consultative selling, no-closing selling, even sensitivity training for salespeople. Most of this seems to get translated to timidity in the field, and to quote Zig Ziglar again, "Timid salespeople have skinny kids."

Today, in teaching and in using Group Presentation Marketing, I often remind myself: "Remember why you're there." I don't care how much they laugh or applaud; whether or not I get a standing ovation is of minor importance. What counts (and all that counts) is the number of people who buy and the amount they buy. These are the real statistics, the real measurements of success.

In fact, I'll tell you a "secret" about speaking that very few pros like to admit: It's surprisingly easy to get an audience to laugh, to applaud, even to get a standing ovation. You can be a mediocre speaker and still engineer those results. So the speaker who takes great pride in "audience ratings" is either foolish or pretentious. In contrast, it's a lot harder to get 70%, 80%, even 90% of the people in an audience to reach into their pockets, pull out their hard-earned money, and spend it on your materials. To accomplish that, you have to deliver a greater quantity of better quality information with greater skill and charisma in order to get those results than you do just to get applause.

Over the last few years, I've appeared on publicly promoted seminar programs with Zig Ziglar, in several dozen U.S. and Canadian cities, with several thousand people in each audience. As the third and last speaker, with only the 4:00 p.m. to 5:00 p.m. time slot to work with, I routinely sell $20,000 to $35,000 worth of my books and cassettes each time. How? *Because I am totally focused on one objective and one objective only: making sales.* Every word, every story in my presentation has been carefully chosen and assembled to make sales. The only measurement of my success I am interested in or pay any attention to is the number of sales.

The reason very few speakers ever become top performers in Group Presentation Marketing, why very few salespeople become high performers in their fields, is because they avoid putting themselves totally on the line for instant, measurable results. In the business of selling, the most significant sales are made after the seventh or eighth call-back to the customer or client. I say this has a lot more to do with the salesperson than with the customer. It is the salesperson's reluctance to push for definite results that causes this statistic.

Most salespeople like to make themselves feel good by having a lot of "almost persuaded" prospects they're working on and calling back on. But not me. I'd much rather have a no than a maybe. I'd rather know where I stand as quickly as possible, so that I can move on to the next potentially productive use of my time. When somebody says to me, "Let me think about it," I say:

- Let's think about it together, out loud. After all, two heads are better than one.

- What, specifically, do you need time to think about?

- When someone has to think over a decision like this, it usually means he or she doesn't yet have enough information with which to make a decision. Let's review what we do know to see what may be missing.

I push to get on with it, right then.

These days, in selling my own services as a speaker or as a consultant, as quickly as possible I open my schedule and say, "Let's see if I can even fit you in this month" or "Do you have a date in mind? Over half of mine for the rest of the year are already booked." I'm "closing" in this way from the very start.

Those who insist on thinking things over present to you just one more challenge: to determine whether or not you know why you're there, and whether or not you're strong enough to get what you wanted. If you are clear on your purpose — for calling someone, meeting with someone, making a presentation — you'll have a big competitive edge over most of the rest of the world. Just having an agenda is a big step forward!

7
STRATEGY #7:
DO EXPECTATIONS GOVERN RESULTS?

It was a big surprise to me when I first discovered that many people actually go into situations expecting to lose. I've learned to expect to win.

My friend Brendan Suhr, now an assistant head coach with Chuck Daly for the Orlando Magic, was asked, back when he and Daly coached the then dominant Detroit Pistons, what the big difference was between them and other NBA teams. Brendan said that, unlike other organizations he'd been with, everybody with the Pistons genuinely and whole-heartedly expected to win every game.

That's an attitude I've taken into my own businesses. Before I moved to Arizona, I had an ad agency and I worked closely with James Tolleson on several of his projects. One project was running a mail-order business; another, a seminar company; and another, raising capital for the expansion of the mail-order business. At any one time, I was working with the people selling seminar enrollments over the phone. At other times, I was recruiting financial backers. In those situations, James' customary parting instruction as either he or I left the office was "Get the check!"

What's more important is what he did *not* say:

- Good *luck* getting the check,
- I *hope* you get the check, or
- *Try* to get the check.

He said *Get* the check because he expected the check to be gotten; the sale to be closed.

I don't think most salespeople expect to "get the check" every time out. Many people respond to an unsuccessful effort by saying, "I didn't expect that to happen anyway." I say, "Then why did you waste any effort on it? If you don't honestly expect success today, why not just roll over and go back to sleep?"

Dan Kennedy's Truth About Selling #6
Super-successful salespeople expect
successful results.

But let's be clear about this: I'm not talking about groundless, unreasonable expectations built out of "positive thinking" and nothing else. I'm talking about expecting success because you've created *reasons* to expect success.

Here's how I approach a selling or negotiating situation. First, I anticipate the worst — and carefully think through the ways that I may be able to counter or overcome the predictable, possible obstacles. Then, I expect the best. Often I visualize the entire process, rehearsing the entire dialogue in my head once, twice, even several times before actually proceeding with the meeting. I sell myself on the likelihood of getting what I want.

Recently, in selling a division of one of my companies to a competitor, I used this process. I thought through all the reasons why it made good sense for them to accept the proposition — from their point of view. By the time I sat down with them in the first meeting I had every expectation of successfully consummating the deal. In fact, I was a little surprised when I walked out without a definite yes and had to wait a couple of weeks to complete the transaction. I feel that my strong positive expectations helped me more calmly and persuasively influence them.

This concept is described by Napoleon Hill in his book *Think and Grow Rich:* "Whatever the mind of man can conceive and *believe*, it can achieve." (Emphasis is mine.)

Believe is the key word in this equation. You have to believe your proposition before anyone else will. And I am convinced that when your belief reaches 100%, you are guaranteed acceptance by the other person — the customer, client, whomever.

Persuasion involves transferring your feelings onto the other person. If you "secretly" feel —

- I'm not very good at persuading others

- He's too smart to fall for this

- She'll never go for this

- He's a much better, much more experienced negotiator

- I wish this problem didn't exist with this deal

- I hope she hasn't gotten a quote from XYZ, too; I can't beat their prices —

then you'll "transmit" those feelings to the other person, and it could affect the response. He or she may become uncomfortable, hesitant, insecure, and reluctant to proceed. And he or she may not consciously know why either, saying, "It's just a feeling."

On the other hand, when you do feel that the proposition is at least as good for the other party as it is for you, when you feel that the other person would be smart to say yes and stupid to say no, when you feel that you have something to offer that is better than anything available from any other source, and when you feel that you are as good at communicating all of that as anyone could possibly be — you transfer those feelings, too.

There are many professional salespeople with tremendous ability, extensive knowledge of their products, good selling skills, comprehensive training and education, and excellent opportunities who fail miserably, repetitively. Why? There is just one ingredient missing in their situation: conviction — the belief in themselves and their proposition.

I'll say it again. The "magic promise" of virtually irresistible persuasive power: When your BELIEF reaches 100%, you are GUARANTEED ACCEPTANCE by the other person.

8

STRATEGY #8:
PROOF: THE MOST IMPORTANT
TOOL FOR EXCEPTIONAL SUCCESS
IN SELLING

I am about to reveal to you — and attempt to sell you on — the single most important, most powerful selling tool that exists. That's a big claim. I know that. Yet I have personally seen this single tool transform losing businesses into huge successes, and mediocre salespeople into superstars. I have used it myself many different times, many different ways, for great profit.

First, a story:

One afternoon I was visiting the offices of a famous, very successful criminal attorney. He and several of his associates were gathered in the firm's conference room discussing a trial that was to begin the following day. He was asking his associates for their comments about their ability to win their client's acquittal.

The client had the risk of serving at least 20 years, possibly longer, in a federal prison should these lawyers fail. In the client's favor was the fact that this particular lawyer very rarely lost a case.

The attorney asked his associates for their comments, and a young lawyer spoke up: "I'm confident that we have gathered enough proof for you to prove his innocence if necessary."

The attorney came up out of his chair, lunged across the conference table, grabbed his young associate by the neck, and pulled him out of his chair, so that they were almost nose-to-nose. He then said, in a deadly voice: "Don't ever send me into a courtroom with 'enough' proof. I want a *preponderance* of proof."

I have never forgotten the importance of that lesson. Having a preponderance of proof makes it possible to sell with 100% effectiveness, 100% of the time. If you want to win with every presentation of every proposition, make sure you have an overwhelming *amount* of proof that what you are selling is a great deal, have an overwhelming *quality* of proof, and have proof that is solidly influential.

PROOF THROUGH TESTIMONIALS

I have recently been working on an advertising, direct-mail, and cable TV campaign for an audiocassette program that helps people lose weight and stay slim without fad diets, without going hungry, without pills, and without an exercise program. (The product really works, by the way.) In presenting it to the public, I want to use an overwhelming quantity of proof, quality of proof, and influential proof.

One effective form of proof is the use of testimonials. I want testimonials from people who have used this product, lost weight, kept weight off, and reaped all sorts of benefits as a result: improved sex life, better health, a promotion at work, etc.

Getting testimonials isn't difficult — anybody can do it. When a sales representative for the insurance sales company created by W. Clement Stone called on a small business owner, he had a huge three-ring notebook full of letters from other business owners who had already acquired a policy and were satisfied with their purchase. Some letters stressed satisfaction with service, others mentioned the low, competitive premium rates, and others mentioned the financing. The first time I saw that presentation, I was in awe: it was overwhelmingly convincing. How could all those people be wrong?

For my project, I wanted, first, a lot of these testimonials. I wanted quantity. An overwhelming amount. Second, I wanted quality testimonials: good, clear writing that got to the point. I wanted permission to use the person's full name, city of residence, age, and occupation. Third, I wanted influential testimonials from people in respected jobs: doctors, lawyers, professional athletes, and executives of well-known companies. Nothing I or the product's inventor would say could ever have the same impact as these testimonials.

Dan Kennedy's Truth About Selling #7
What others say about you and your product, service, or business is at least 1,000 times more convincing than what you say, even if you are 1,000 times more eloquent.

Testimonial letters and comments can be used in sales and marketing in many different ways. They can be used in advertising, direct mail, and promotional literature. They can be used as part of a one-on-one or group sales presentation, like the insurance sales rep used his. They can be given to the client to read. They can be put in a big notebook and kept in the waiting room or reception area for people to browse through.

In my experience, there is nothing more valuable than a great testimonial letter — other than two great testimonial letters!

A PICTURE IS WORTH A THOUSAND WORDS

Another incredibly powerful type of proof is pictorial. The cliché is true: a picture is worth a thousand words. Pictorial proof is interesting and novel, it communicates at a glance, and it has lasting impact. Your camera could be your best friend in sales!

Ira Hayes, a former top National Cash Register (NCR) salesman, used this technique when he was selling. He had a 20- to 30-foot black fabric panel that he carried with him. On that panel were thousands of snapshots of happy, satisfied customers standing next to their shiny new cash register. Hayes would take this giant "wall" of snapshots into a prospect's office and unfurl it impressively. The sale was made before the selling even started — because the proof was overwhelming.

Ira was once asked, when he was traveling and speaking for NCR, why NCR and he were so willing to reveal his selling secret. Ira answered: "We're not worried about our competitor's salespeople stealing this idea. We can't even get our own people to use it."

I've only seen one other salesperson use it to a similar extent: Bill Glazner, a Ford salesman in Phoenix. He is, in my opinion, the best, most professional automobile salesperson in the business — and I have met many others. In his cubicle, the walls are covered with snapshots, each showing a customer or a customer-family, smiling, standing next to their new Ford. Each photo is dated and has the customer's name on it. My wife's photo is there, with her LTD Crown Victoria. My photo is there, with my Lincoln. My brother's photo is there with his pickup truck. My father's photo is there, with his Mercury Marquis. Some families have many more photos there, from a series of vehicles they purchased over the years. It doesn't take too long to accept the pictures as proof that Glazner treats his customers right — otherwise, how could he have so many of them?

You can use "photo proof" in any type of business. A retail store might take pictures of happy customers with their newly purchased merchandise. A lawn service company might photograph the customers' yards and gardens. A florist might photograph the happy, surprised recipients of delivered flowers. In my literature, I often use the photos taken of me with famous people: actors and actresses such as Florence Henderson, Gloria Loring, and Gil Gerard; TV hosts such as Robb Weller; and sports personalities such as Fran Tarkenton and the late Don Drysdale. Give some thought to how you can apply this principle to your business.

STATISTICAL PROOF

Statistics provide a third impressive form of proof. For example, we surveyed a group of entrepreneurs who were using our audiocassette materials last year, and we now show the survey results to new customers. The results conclude that:

- 98% reported satisfaction
- 83% reported improved sales
- 87% made additional purchases

Sometimes, putting your statistical proof in chart or bar graph format can make it easier for people to understand.

OTHER PROOF

Consider these ideas for evidence you might use:

- Customer or client lists
- Length of time in business
- Past credentials, qualifications, experience
- Financial references
- Number of cities/countries serviced
- Number of customers served

HOW MUCH PROOF IS ENOUGH?
HOW MUCH PROOF IS TOO MUCH?

There is no such thing as enough; no such thing as too much. It is better to have more than you need rather than less.

I can't tell you how many salespeople and businesspeople I have taught this to, *yet it is still a well-kept secret.* We can't get the salespeople in our own companies to use these ideas. No one else at the car dealership where Bill Glazner works will use the ideas, even though he has been a star, award-winning, high-income performer. Why not? Maybe other salespeople are lazy. Maybe they have low self-esteem that prevents them from excelling. Maybe they think the concept won't work in their line of work.

It's not your job, though, to worry about why others won't use these techniques. Their resistance is your opportunity! Successful people do the things that unsuccessful people are unwilling to do. If you choose to join the successful minority, you'll discover that most of the things you do to get results — even if openly shared with others — will rarely be copied and used by others. For that reason, the use of preponderance of proof as the core of selling or advertising or marketing remains a best-kept, immensely valuable secret.

9
STRATEGY #9:
FRED HERMAN'S K.I.S.S. PRINCIPLE

Earl Nightingale once called Fred Herman "America's greatest sales trainer." It's a title I think he deserved. To my knowledge, Fred is the only salesman ever to appear as a guest on "The Tonight Show" with Johnny Carson. (Carson said, "Okay, since you're the great salesman, sell me this ashtray." Fred picked it up, examined it, and asked, "If you were going to buy this ashtray, what would you expect to pay for it?" Carson named a price. Fred said, "Sold!")

I discovered Fred Herman's work after I already had years of experience in selling; I wish I had found it when I started! Fred is probably most famous for coining the KISS Principle for Selling: KEEP IT SIMPLE, SALESMAN! This is an immensely valuable lesson that I learned the hard way.

In my first sales position, with the publishing company I described earlier in this book, one of the things I was most effective at was opening new accounts where we could place the entire six-foot-tall spinner rack. The standard procedure prescribed by the company was to review the catalogue of books with the buyer, choosing the titles to be displayed in the rack. As the rack only held about one-third of all the available titles, this selection process was a time-consuming chore. The customer and I had to discuss just about every title. Inevitably, he or she wanted more variety than the rack could accommodate. I found it took almost two hours, on average, to place a new rack.

Then I realized that almost 90% of the racks I placed carried the same titles on them. So I reasoned that I knew better than the customer which titles would do best, and I was wasting his or her time and mine discussing products that would not be on the rack. From this realization, I created a "standard rack assortment" which I copied and used every time I sold a new customer a rack. All the customer had to do was initial the precompleted form and I was on my way. Average time savings: 90 minutes per new rack placement!

How come nobody else in the company had thought of this? People have an incredible tendency to complicate their lives. I'm not sure why that happens, but I know that it happens. I even have a name for it: complexity creep. Complexity just creeps up on you when you're not looking. And, unnecessary complexity creates a whole host of problems. It wastes time, it drains your energy and enthusiasm, it often confuses the customer — and confused customers do not buy!

YOU CAN GET RICH MAKING THE COMPLICATED SIMPLE

I recently saw an interesting advertisement placed by a copywriter looking for work. He billed himself as a "professional explainer" who specialized in "making complicated things simple and easy to understand." That's exactly what you need to do in your efforts to persuade others.

Not long ago, I was wrestling with a direct-mail project involving the sale of a rather complicated financial product to essentially unsophisticated investors. Two consecutive test mailings failed miserably. I thought they were well-written, clear, and exciting. I thought they offered a great deal to the customer. I thought everything was right. Just one small problem: they didn't work. I read through them a hundred times and still found no clue to the problem. One evening, I got the idea to add a little diagram at the end of the literature that showed — in cartoon form — the gist of the product. The addition of this little drawing, which showed visually what was said in the copy, made the piece a huge success. The mailing with the drawing got phenomenally good results. That one little drawing made the complicated simple and understandable.

P.T. Barnum once said that "No man ever went broke overestimating the ignorance of the American public." Maybe that judgment of the American consumer is a little harsh and cynical, but it does introduce a major mistake made by the majority of sales and marketing people over and over again: overestimating the sophistication of their customers.

It's natural for you to insist that the people you deal with are smarter than everybody else's customers. That reflects well on you, doesn't it? It's good for your ego to think that you're dealing with a "better class" of people. It may be good for the ego, but it's bad for the bank account! Here is the best way to succeed in advertising, selling, marketing, or persuading others (regardless of who they are or how smart and sophisticated you believe they are): present *everything* in the simplest possible language and in the simplest possible form.

10

SELL MONEY AT A DISCOUNT

When you fully understand the technique of selling money at a discount and can find a way to apply it to your product, service, or business, you will have created a bottomless gold mine! (I'll admit, though, that it's not the easiest technique to apply universally.)

I was once retained as a consultant to an individual who lectured on methods of preventing theft from employees and vendors' delivery staff. This individual was a reformed thief who knew how it was done from having done it! (This kind of theft is a little-known problem of huge magnitude. In the typical convenience store, for example, the theft equals or even exceeds the owner's profit!)

This expert ex-thief was teaching business owners how to prevent this sort of loss — and they were thrilled. In fact, he had boxes full of testimonial letters from store owners and executives citing specific amounts of money saved in the weeks or months following his seminar. These letters documented the saving of thousands of dollars per store. Some big companies reported savings of as much as $100,000 in just a couple of months by applying what they learned.

He had no idea what he was worth! He was charging only $500 to conduct his all-day seminar, and he had one little reference notebook with six audiocassettes that recapped the seminar, simply packaged in a bag, that he was selling for about $30.

Let me confess: this was the easiest marketing task I ever had. The first thing I suggested was that he raise his fees. In fact, I convinced him to triple his fee from $500 to $1,500 immediately. To his shock (but not mine) there was very little protest and no loss of clients. Shortly after that, the fee was raised again to $2,500 with just a little client grumbling. Even at $2,500 a day, he was such a bargain that no one could afford to grumble too much. In essence, we were now selling $10,000 to $100,000 cash for $2,500. Who wouldn't buy that? And we had the proof to demonstrate it.

I based his entire marketing program on proving that he was offering money at a discount. In other words, we showed the prospect such a large, compelling return on investment that he or she couldn't say no, regardless of the price.

Right now, I know a consultant in the field of real estate mortgages who guarantees to help clients save at least $10,000 over the life of their home mortgages without increasing the amount of the monthly payments. He requires a fee of $2,000 for his service, paid as soon as he has arranged and demonstrated the savings to the client. Well, who wouldn't agree to that deal?

That's the kind of money-at-a-discount "picture" you somehow have to engineer and present for your product or service. The same basic principle applies to negotiating other types of financial transactions. You can sell just about any business if you can show the buyer how the business (not the buyer) pays for the purchase.

You may never come across a situation where that demonstration is as clear-cut as it was with my client in the theft control business. I know I haven't come across another such situation. But the technique can be applied, to some degree, to most businesses. It may take some long, hard thought, some research, and some patience, but I assure you it's worth all that and more.

HOW TO PUT MONEY IN THEIR POCKETS AND THEN SET IT ON FIRE

You've undoubtedly heard the saying "his money's burning a hole in his pocket." It's used to describe people who can't keep their hands off their money; they can't wait to spend it. I've done a lot of selling by first putting money in the prospect's pocket, then setting it on fire. You can too. Let me explain.

When I sold millions of dollars of Cassette Learning Systems to doctors in evening seminars, the seminars were free but the doctors had to post a $25 deposit to guarantee they would show up; the deposit was "refundable" at the end of the seminar. After presenting the "commercial" and closing the sale, I'd do a "Columbo" — a sales technique named after the rumpled raincoat character played by Peter Falk, famous for saying "Just one more thing…." I would say: "Oh, just one more thing, you'll recall you paid a $25 deposit to guarantee you'd be here this evening, and you've kept that promise, so your $25 *is* refundable. And we'll double that refund right before your very eyes; we'll match it with $25 of our money, so you can deduct $50 from your System purchase this evening. Just cross out the $499 price, deduct the $50, and write $449 on your form."

Even with an audience that many would argue was too sophisticated for such a strategy, this worked magically. What I did was put $50 into their pockets and then set it on fire. If they didn't buy a System, they "lost" that $50, and that hurt!

I've replicated this strategy in other group sales situations, in person-to-person selling, even in direct-mail campaigns.

General Motors and Ford are using a version of this idea with their "private label" Visa and MasterCard. With the Ford card, you accumulate "rebate dollars" for using the card, but those dollars are good only toward the purchase of a Ford vehicle. If you use that one Ford Visa for all your credit card purchases, you might accumulate $2,000 to $3,000 in "rebate dollars." With that money burning a hole in your pocket, is there any way you'll "lose it" and buy another brand of car? I don't think so.

CREATING VALUE FROM THIN AIR AND ADDING VALUE TO EVERY OFFER

Rene Gnam, a top direct-response advertising consultant, invites his clients to come to Florida and stay in the guest house at his "Response Ranch," not just for the day of consultation, but for a couple of extra days of relaxation and recreation. He provides the use of a car, a fully-stocked refrigerator, and the obvious opportunity to take the entire air travel expense as a business tax deduction.

When I sell my Cassette Learning Systems that have to do with advertising and marketing, I always include several "critique coupons" that entitle the person to send me their ads, brochures, or sales letters for my personal, written mini-report: an analysis of what they've done effectively and what could be done better. This is called a "second opinion consultation," for which I usually charge $100 to $200, depending on the complexity of the piece being reviewed. In other words, each of these coupons has a minimum value of $100. With a Learning System that I sell at many seminars for $278, I include three coupons, so the customer gets $300 of added value with a $278 purchase! (A sample of the coupon is shown on the next page.) You might want to use this idea in your business and sales.

We go even farther with the travel newsletter one of my companies publishes. With a year's subscription for $89 to *The Insight Travel Letter*, we give a bonus travel club membership and incentive package worth over $500. There are hundreds of dollars of air travel rebates, half-price hotel discounts, restaurant coupons, and a lot more.

You can create value through premiums, guarantees and warranties, special services, frequent-user rebates — turn your imagination loose and find an opportunity that matches your particular business.

SAMPLE CRITIQUE COUPON*

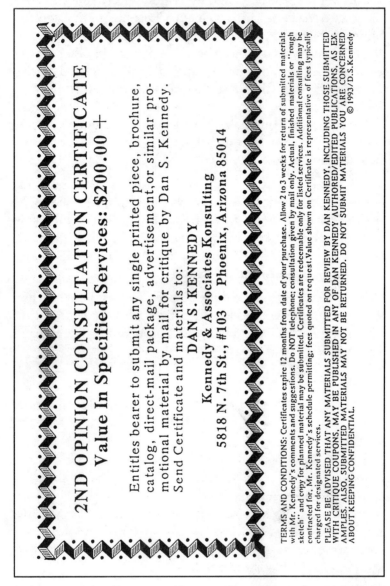

2ND OPINION CONSULTATION CERTIFICATE
Value In Specified Services: $200.00 +

Entitles bearer to submit any single printed piece, brochure, catalog, direct-mail package, advertisement, or similar promotional material by mail for critique by Dan S. Kennedy. Send Certificate and materials to:

DAN S. KENNEDY
Kennedy & Associates Konsulting
5818 N. 7th St., #103 • Phoenix, Arizona 85014

TERMS AND CONDITIONS: Certificates expire 12 months from date of your purchase. Allow 2 to 3 weeks for return of submitted materials with Mr. Kennedy's comments and suggestions. Do NOT telephone; consultation given by mail only. Actual, finished materials or "rough sketch" and copy for planned material may be submitted. Certificates are redeemable only for listed services. Additional consulting may be contracted for. Mr. Kennedy's schedule permitting; fees quoted on request. Value shown on Certificate is representative of fees typically charged for designated services.

PLEASE BE ADVISED THAT ANY MATERIALS SUBMITTED FOR REVIEW BY DAN KENNEDY, INCLUDING THOSE SUBMITTED WITH CRITIQUE COUPONS, MAY BE PUBLISHED IN ANY OF DAN KENNEDY AUTHORED/EDITED PUBLICATIONS, AS EXAMPLES. ALSO, SUBMITTED MATERIALS MAY NOT BE RETURNED. DO NOT SUBMIT MATERIALS YOU ARE CONCERNED ABOUT KEEPING CONFIDENTIAL.

© 1993/D.S.Kennedy

* A bonus to readers: You can use this coupon. To avoid destroying your book, just make a photocopy, fill it out, and send it to the author. But make only one copy — we track the usage so multiple copies will be refused!

11
STRATEGY #11:
ALWAYS COMPARE APPLES
TO ORANGES

"You can't compare apples to oranges." I'm sure you've heard that; I encourage you to get it completely out of your mind! The secret to eliminating price resistance *is* to compare apples to oranges! Let me give you an example:

From 1983 to 1985, I built the largest integrated publishing and seminar business exclusively serving chiropractors and dentists in North America. In my seminars for SuccessTrak Inc., I sold a 12-month "trak" (subscription) of audiocassettes on practice promotion and success subjects. Counting the bonus items, there were 18 cassettes in the one-year program — sold for $499.

But most audiocassette albums, available on a variety of topics, sell for an average of $10 a tape. On that basis, these 18 cassettes would sell for only $180. The economics of marketing via free seminars required that we sell for the considerably higher price. Also, due to the specialized, valuable nature of the information in these cassettes, we felt justified in commanding the higher price. But how do you clearly and successfully justify that price to the consumer? Obviously, if you compare other cassette products to these cassette products (apples to apples), you're dead.

In this case, we compared cassettes to seminars. If the participants obtained the same basic information that was in the cassettes by attending the seminars on which the cassettes were based, they would have spent over $780 on enrollment fees alone, not to mention time away from their practices during the week or family on weekends, travel and lodging costs, and other expenses. All things considered, by buying the tapes people could save much more than $300!

By switching to an apples-to-oranges comparison, I presented a compelling argument of savings to the consumer.

Keep in mind that most of the advice you get about dealing with price resistance is wrong. If you deal with price resistance by arguing in favor of your higher quality, your better service, etc., you will find your sales work difficult most of the time. People do want superior quality goods and services, but they still don't enjoy paying premium prices for them. Many marketers fight that battle unnecessarily.

It is much easier and much more effective to switch the standards of comparison; win by comparing apples to oranges and then "throw in" the superior quality at "no extra cost."

If you are in a selling situation where there is heads-on competition, even competitive bidding, this technique can still be used. Recently I was consulting with a manufacturing company in direct competitive bid warfare with a lower-price opponent. My client was losing bid after bid. I said: "Something has to change here." They said: "It can't. We can't cut our prices any lower." I said: "If we can't come in with the lower bid, we might as well come in with an even higher bid — but let's change the rules of the game when we do it."

The savvy sales pro learns to alter the "rules of the game" to give himself or herself an overwhelming advantage. Forget all about "playing fair." Forget all about competing on a "level playing field." These are clichés that are best lasered out of your consciousness. All your life, you've been told to "play fair," and that conditioning of your subconscious may be holding you back now. Selling in competitive situations is all about finding or inventing an *unfair* advantage for yourself. Go ahead and make it impossible for your competitors to keep up with you.

That's exactly the approach I took with this client. I analyzed their operations and discovered that they were in a position to include warehousing and fulfillment at a much lower cost than their competitor could possibly do. By adding that service to their specifications, their higher quote became the more attractive quote.

Many big companies have learned this lesson, although they don't capitalize on it to the extent they could. In traveling, for example, I prefer to stay in an embassy suite if available. These are two-room suites with free cocktails and a free, full breakfast "built into" their room rates. In reality, their suites aren't much bigger than a full-size hotel room; they've just creatively apportioned and partitioned the space. By changing the standards of comparison, though, they have a product that is much more attractive to many people than their competitors. They have created a suite versus a room at the same price comparison.

In my Millionaire-Maker Day Seminars, I teach people to "reinvent" their products and services so that they make direct price comparisons impossible. It's the smart sales pro who steps back from day-to-day activities, mentally takes a very deep breath, and is able to look at his or her products or services with fresh eyes.

There are many different ways to change the rules of the game and use apples-to-oranges comparisons. I urge you to look for ways appropriate to your selling activities. This is the price resistance eliminator!

12

STRATEGY #12:
IN SEARCH OF
THE FREE LUNCH

There's an old story about the king who commissioned a group of the brightest scholars in his kingdom to assemble the wisdom of the ages. They first came back with a truckload full of stone tablets. He told them to condense and simplify. They came with an encyclopedia. He demanded that they condense and simplify. Finally, ultimately, they returned with a single sentence: there's no such thing as a free lunch.

Every sane, sensible, logical person knows that to be the truth. However, we all still love to believe there might be! That's why premiums work so well in selling. A premium is a free gift or a free bonus: something the buyer gets free when purchasing something else. Everything from books to Buicks have been given away at one time or another as a premium with a purchase.

I personally love to use premiums in selling. I've given away cameras, vacation trips, books, reports, subscriptions, collectors' art prints, free consulting services, jewelry, and many other things in personal, group, and mail-order selling over the years. Here are some tips on using premiums:

- Don't give away the same things you sell. In most cases, this is a bad practice because it devalues your merchandise or services.

- Offer premiums that people want for themselves. Even if you're in the business-to-business marketing environment, it's best to offer a luxury personal-use item.

- Give away things people want but rarely buy for themselves. I've found that people will often buy something as a premium that they ordinarily would never buy on its own.

- Make the premium relevant to your offer or to your customers or clients.

When I was consulting with a publishing company, I put together a direct-mail campaign for a line of their programs with the theme "Success comes in cans, not in cannot's." For the premium, we offered a little baby-food can with the "success comes in cans" label. The campaign was extremely successful, which I am certain had much more to do with the customers' desire for the premium than for the product. Consider this:

- More than 80% of the customers ordering by phone made a point of asking about the premium to make sure they would get it.

- More than 30% of the purchasers asked about getting extra "cans" for friends or associates.

- A large number of inquiries were received from people who wanted to buy the can labels, but not the programs advertised in the mailing.

It goes to show that people do respond to desirable premium offers, and premiums can even drive the sale.

HOW TO CLOSE THE DIFFICULT SALE
WITH A VERY DESIRABLE PREMIUM

For many years, the direct selling companies in the home security and fire alarm systems businesses have relied on desirable premiums. Although everybody needs and should have a fire alarm system in their home, nobody wants one, and so it is a difficult sale. Typically, these companies will offer a beautiful set of crystal and dinnerware, or a gorgeous collection of jewelry, or an all-expenses-paid vacation as the free bonus gift, to close the sale. This lets the buyers get something they really *want* while doing the right thing and purchasing something they really *need.* The gift may very well be something they would never buy for themselves, but they love the opportunity of getting it "free."

HOW TO STRENGTHEN CUSTOMER LOYALTY AND
STIMULATE REFERRALS WITH PREMIUMS

Premiums can also be used to build customer loyalty and stimulate word-of-mouth advertising. When my favorite car salesman delivered the last Lincoln-Continental I bought, he called my attention to a little Auto Butler decal on the window. Anytime during the first year I have the car, if I have a flat tire, dead battery, lock my keys in the car, or have some other problem, I can call the Auto Butler and they'll come fix the problem — free. This was not promised to me as an inducement to buy the car; I didn't find out about it until he delivered the car. But I've since told at least a dozen people about it. Why? Like anybody else, I like to brag about getting a good deal.

The month I was finishing writing this book, Federal Express launched an advertising campaign based around a frequent-user reward program — FedExtras — enabling their steady customers to accumulate points toward office machines, other business products and services, and even travel incentives. But you don't have to be a big business to use such a strategy. My chiropractor has a wall display featuring several different health products, a popular exercise device, even a package of movie tickets. You can choose one as your gift when you refer two patients to the practice. Does it work? Fabulously well.

PREMIUMS AND "BIG TICKET SELLING"

You can even use premiums in negotiating. With one big consulting contract I closed, I "threw in" a complete library of my books and audiocassette programs. The retail value was well over $2,500, but the cost to me was less than $300. I once gave away a certain amount of consulting time to an individual, for his business, as a "bonus" for his investing in one of my companies. In selling a business, I included consulting time as a bonus. I know a businessman who secured the services of a top lawyer by including free use of a private plane in the agreement in addition to the normal retainers and fees.

You can use the "free lunch technique" many different ways in business. Do not make the mistake of overlooking or discounting how powerful and universal the appeal of this approach is.

13

STRATEGY #13:
THE MAGIC OF MYSTIQUE

Part of the value of what someone does lies in how difficult others think it is to do. For example, in America, people say that public speaking is their number one fear. Incredibly, more people are afraid of speaking in public than of getting cancer, having a prolonged illness, or even dying! To me, however, public speaking has become just about the easiest thing I know how to do. I know, though, that I command a significant amount of respect from a group before I even speak a word, just by virtue of doing what they feel is so terrifyingly difficult to do. It is much, much harder to speak to a group of other professional speakers because to them there is no mystique in the speaking.

People wouldn't pay to see a magician perform if they knew exactly how the magic tricks were done. Remove the mystique and there's no product left. And that's true of most things. In sales and marketing it's important to create and preserve some mystique, glamour, intrigue, and uniqueness.

PERCEPTION IS REALITY:
THE "STORY" IS THE "SECRET INGREDIENT"

McDonald's special sauce. The formula for Coca-Cola. Colonel Sanders' secret recipe. These things preserve some mystique in otherwise mundane products.

Nowhere is this more visibly at work than in the cosmetics and skin-care products field. If you haven't paid much attention to this business, the next time you're at a department store, stroll slowly past the cosmetic counters. You will be astounded at how many different brand names, colors, scents, and mystifying products there are. The ingredients are incredible: dew collected only from tulips growing on the sunny side of the Swiss Alps, even sheep sperm!

Yet, as much as the consumers of these products hate hearing this, all of it is pretty much the same. In fact, there's only one manufacturer for every 50 to 100 different brands, labels, and product lines — all with the same ingredients, the only significant differences being the packaging, price, and "story."

If you took away the mystique created by the stories, the celebrities, and the advertising, you'd have one generic line of cosmetics, warranting price points 50% to 500% less than today's going rates. But nobody would buy it, and everybody would hate you for telling how the magician did the trick.

CREATING YOUR OWN MYSTIQUE

Developing the mystique is possible for anyone. One technique is what I call "Takeaway Selling," which is explored in detail in Part 4 of this book. Learning to use Takeaway Selling has had greater impact on my personal earnings than any other single thing I've ever discovered or learned, so be sure to study this section of the book. You'll find that some of the ideas regarded as "gospel" about success in selling are challenged.

Another "trick" is to create your own mystique terminology for what you do, just as the cosmetic manufacturers do. In our self-improvement industry, the hugely successful EST program built mystique around its unique language and terminology. In EST, you only know if you have "it" when you've got "it" and otherwise you can't understand what "it" is. EST's Werner

Erhard learned this mystique-creating tactic from his earlier experiences in Mind Dynamics, the human potential seminar arm of the controversial cosmetic sales/pyramid marketing company, Holiday Magic. At introductory seminars for such programs, those already "in" would be talking enthusiastically and happily with one another in a language largely incomprehensible by the new guests. Because "outsiders" are naturally motivated to become "insiders," this situation alone helped sell these programs.

Mystique can be perpetuated, and a desire to become a part of what's going on can be created with a language of your own. The computer industry has done a spectacular job on this — maybe even an excessive job!

ANYONE CAN CREATE PERSONAL MYSTIQUE

There's mystique value in certain personal skills anyone can master if it is made a priority. Salespeople with phenomenal memory skills, for example, have a competitive edge.

I have shared the platform with several different memory trainers over the years, and, in every case, audiences are fascinated, impressed, and motivated by the demonstrations of phenomenal memory skills. Harry Lorayne, arguably America's foremost memory expert, can stand at the entrance to an auditorium, meet 100 people — even 200 — for the first time and, hours later, go from one to another and correctly call them by name. These people have shown me their "processes," and, although I have not taken the time to do it, I am convinced anybody can learn and master these skills. You can use these skills to remember names and faces, complex technical or financial data, and details of presentations without notes. It could be your path to personal mystique.

MODERN TECHNOLOGY
CAN CONFER MYSTIQUE

You might be able to use "amazing" technology in your selling activities. There's an insurance salesperson I know who has a small, portable computer and fax machine that he carries with him, which he hooks up to the client's phone. As he interviews the client, he enters all the vital statistics (e.g., age, income, retirement savings goal), then transmits it back to another computer at his office. Minutes later, back through his fax machine, a printout of a personalized insurance plan for that client arrives. It has bar graphs, charts, tables, and is very impressive.

NOTHING BEATS A
"MAGICAL" DEMONSTRATION

Can your product be used in a particularly "amazing" demonstration? I recently produced a TV infomercial about a portable "engraving system," and to demonstrate how safe and easy it is, potential customers were invited to engrave a design on an eggshell, without breaking the egg.

One of the items that has sold very successfully at state fairs is the chamois cloth that soaks up a whole gallon of spilled Coca-Cola. It's amazing! How does it do that?

HOW TO UNMASK AND
STILL CREATE MYSTIQUE

I recommend developing and sustaining some level of mystique in your business, too. If everybody knows everything about your business, you'll often wind up with no business! Yet, sometimes, you can gain by revealing rather than concealing.

Several years ago, I wrote a book — *The Ultimate Sales Letter*, still available in bookstores — in which I reveal and demonstrate each of the 28 steps that I go through as a professional direct-response copywriter to create powerful sales letters or ads for my clients — at fees starting at $3,850 up to as much as $15,000 plus royalties. I revealed every step I take, but still, many people read the book and choose to hire me anyway. Why? Because there's enough intangible creativity in what I do that even when you know the steps of the process, you may not be able to do it as well as I can.

I watched Chuck Daly and Brendan Suhr conduct a practice and a coaching session with the Detroit Pistons, and then coach a big game several years ago. I'm a quick learner, so I think I understand the structure of what they did and why they did it. But I still couldn't duplicate their experience and talent at applying the process. In fact, I left with a greater appreciation for what they do than I had before.

If what you do creates that kind of awe and respect, then you create mystique by revealing your process rather than concealing it.

EVERYTHING OLD IS NEW AGAIN — AT LEAST IT BETTER BE!

One related matter that messes up a lot of people in marketing is "what's new." A sales rep in one of our companies was once overheard complaining that we hadn't introduced any new products for a long time. "Have all your customers seen all of our products?" I asked. The rep freely admitted they had not. "Then you've got new products," I said.

A funny thing occasionally happens in the advertising business: a client will cancel or change an ad campaign that's working perfectly just because they got bored with it and assumed everybody else was, too. That's a bad assumption. There are ad campaigns that sustain success for five, even ten years. These campaigns are old hat to their owners but are new to new customers who are paying attention to them for the first time. If it's unknown to someone, it's a secret — regardless of how routine it may be to you.

I had to learn that in my consulting activities. I charge fees for disclosing knowledge that to me is quite ordinary. To those who need to know and don't, though, it's exotic and valuable. For example, I know quite a bit about how to select and obtain mailing lists for just about any purpose. If you need a list of middle-aged dog owners who live in Philadelphia, subscribe to *Better Homes and Gardens,* and have at least one credit card, I know how to get that list. To me, there's nothing to that. To those who don't know and need to, it's worth thousands of dollars.

Don't overlook the importance and value of this lesson. Think carefully about ways you can apply it to your business. John D. Rockefeller said the best route to a fortune is to glamorize the ordinary. I agree.

14

STRATEGY #14:
I'D RATHER BE DUMB AND PERSISTENT
THAN SMART AND IMPATIENT

I recently closed a sale I'd been nursing along for almost two years. Now, I would have preferred to have gotten the job done 23 months sooner, but sometimes there's just no substitute for building a relationship through repetitive contact over time. Just about everything that is "impossible" becomes possible given sufficient time, patience, and persistence.

A friend of mine tells a story about a dumb frog that fell into a big barrel half full of cream. He was close to drowning, and all the other frogs circled the top of the barrel and laughed and jeered at him. But this frog was so dumb he thought they were cheering him on, so he paddled faster and faster and faster until he churned the cream into butter, and then he was able to hop back out of the barrel.

It's possible to be too smart, to know so much that you know all the reasons why it won't, can't, and shouldn't work. While you are sitting around stymied by all those problems, some dumb frog down the road is doing it!

HOW BEING A DUMB FROG GOT THIS ROOKIE
A VETERAN'S TOP INCOME — FAST

I remember at the very beginning of my speaking career getting cornered at a National Speakers Association workshop by a very successful, very prominent "old pro." He generously explained to me, at great length and in great detail, all "the dues" I would have to pay to "get good" before I could even hope to do well in the business. He painted a rather dreary picture of years of begging for low-paid or even zero-compensation opportunities to speak and gain exposure. He told me that if I made a practice of hanging around guys like him and watching their every move, I might amount to something some day.

Finally, when I could get a word in edgewise, I brought up the subject of money. Instead of talking about the number of different audiences he had spoken to or the number of miles he had traveled, I wanted to hear about money: the only real measurement of the worth of a person, product, or service in the marketplace. I asked how much might I expect to earn in the business. His long-winded answer culminated with: "…as much as $100,000 a year after 10 or 15 years." I said: "Pardon me, but I made $5,000 my first month, and it looks like I'll top $100,000 this year, my first year. I was sort of looking for someone who was really doing a big job."

I don't tell that story to be arrogant or to rub the other guy's nose in it, but rather to illustrate this point: This guy did know all the ropes. He really understood the business inside and out and upside down. Compared to him, I was a dumb frog. And I was going about some things the hard way. (For example, I was selling myself as a speaker door-to-door, business-to-business, in person.) But through ignorance, confidence, patience, and persistence, I was getting spectacular results.

The next time you run into one of these know-it-all "experts" who gives you all the reasons you *can't* succeed, walk away. Who are they — who am I, for that matter — to tell you what you can't do? There's a guy pitching in major league baseball with one arm. I wonder how many people tried "for his own good" to convince him to forget about baseball? The experts in the amusement park business laughed Walt Disney out of a meeting room. Among other things, they told him the idea of having just one entrance and exit for a big park was the dumbest idea of the century. I could fill a book with such stories. The moral of many of them is "persistence pays."

If I had to make a choice between genius and a great capacity for persistence, I'd choose persistence every time. Fortunately, you don't necessarily have to choose one in favor of the other. Instead, you can work at mixing the ingredients together in a balanced formula for success.

You've probably often heard the phrase "work smarter, not harder." Many people take that as an indictment of anybody who works hard. Yet, just about every discovery about how to do something "smart" evolves out of doing it persistently and working hard at it. Call me old-fashioned, but I think hard work is the best path to discovering opportunities to something with less work. I bet the guy who invented the tractor walked behind a few mule teams with a plow first.

DOES SUCCESS — OR FAILURE
— BREED SUCCESS?

In my speaking career of about 20 years, I've built 11 different platform selling presentations for my own use, culminating with the one I've used at all the public seminars with Zig Ziglar and many other engagements for the past three years. Each one has provided me with excellent incomes. Each one, however, started out as a failure. Each one produced unsatisfactory results the first few times I used it, but each of those times, I learned from the audience reactions what was working and what wasn't. Then I adjusted the presentation, delivered it again, observed and learned, adjusted again, until it finally "hit." Fortunately, each successive one has required less of this, thanks to the cumulative experience. Still, it's the willingness to fail and the failure itself that makes success possible.

My friend Ted Nicholas, famous self-publisher and promoter of the bestselling book *How to Form Your Own Corporation Without a Lawyer for Under $75,* has sold over $200 million worth of all of his books through mail-order ads he has written himself. Yet he'll cheerfully tell you that eight out of ten of his ads fail. It's what he learns from these failures that makes it possible for him to create the big winners — direct-response ads that return two, three, four, and even five times their ad cost consistently, month after month, year after year.

Dan Kennedy's Truth About Selling #9
If you're going to arrive at the sales presentation that achieves the maximum possible results, you're going to have to try a lot of different things that flop along the way.

Don't ever mistake genius for persistence. When you look at top achievers in any field, selling included, the temptation is to credit them with genius status, which makes it impossible for an ordinary mortal like yourself to match them. But the truth is, more often than not, their current ability to perform is the result of dogged persistence, not gifted genius, and *that* you can replicate.

15

STRATEGY #15:
PEOPLE ARE DIFFERENT, AND SOME ARE MORE DIFFERENT THAN OTHERS

If you've read many books about selling or listened to many sales trainers, you know that there is a lot of emphasis on "canned," memorized, and practiced sales techniques. The problem with most sales techniques is that they only work well with a fraction of the population. A person with one type of personality will respond differently to the same situation than another person with a different personality.

For decades, the selling profession simply ignored this, believing that there was little to be done about it. In many respects, that attitude is a pretty primitive approach to a process that involves a lot of psychology. Fortunately, there have been some significant scientific advancements in sales training in the past five years, so you can learn to identify your customer's primary personality style and modify your selling style to be more acceptable to that person.

There are sophisticated tests and lengthy seminars you can take to identify your own personality style — and others' — but for the purposes of this book, I'll provide a simple explanation. First, understand that you have a primary personality style, which governs your selling style. Consider these four basic primary personality styles:

(a) *The amiable.* This is the friendly, easygoing person who is likeable and likes to be liked and is very much concerned with what others think about him or her. In selling, this person is prone to accept stalls and objections. He or she doesn't "power" dress, but is concerned with appearance as part of the concern for acceptance of others.

The amiable person, as a customer or client, tends to be agreeable, again out of a concern for being liked. The "relationship factor" is very important to this person.

(b) *The expressive.* This person is the excited, enthusiastic type who uses a lot of gestures and superlatives. He or she may dress, talk, and act a little "loud." The expressive salesperson can be guilty of "hype," but his or her greatest asset is great, visible enthusiasm.

The expressive person as a customer is easily caught up in infectious enthusiasm. He or she responds well to the salesperson's painting of word pictures and likes to interact in the sales process.

(c) *The analytical.* Think of your stereotypical accountant or engineer. He or she is typically a good, logical thinker but a poor communicator with a limited sense of humor. He or she probably isn't a very effective salesperson, except in highly technical fields.

The analytical person as a customer requires and responds to a lot of well-documented, well-organized, factual information and evidence.

(d) *The hard driver.* This is a person who is an impatient, bottom-line oriented, busy, over-committed workaholic who wants it done his or her way yesterday. As a salesperson, the hard driver tends to close more sales on the first call or in the first presentation than any of the other personality styles, but he or she also leaves some scorched earth behind.

The hard-driver as the customer is equally impatient, decisive, even impulsive in the guise of decisiveness.

Although everyone is a mixture of these and other personality types, most people can be identified as having one of these as their primary personality style.

As a salesperson, you must recognize that there are natural conflicts between these personality styles. If you are a hard driver, as I am, you will tend to offend, irritate, and even frighten an analytical person. And, vice versa, if you are an analytical person, you'll find it tough to sell to a hard driver because you'll provide all sorts of information he or she could care less about.

The last time I bought a new car I picked it out in under 15 minutes. I wanted to get on to the next matter. A few days later, I went to the same car showroom with a friend. He has a more balanced personality than I do, and has pronounced analytical and amiable tendencies. As a result, it took over an hour for him to pick out his car. He checked things I never bothered to look at. He test drove the car; I did not. And he carried on a friendly, sociable conversation with the salesperson, whereas my conversation was strictly limited to the deal.

Dan Kennedy's Truth About Selling #10
If you try to sell to everyone without
consciously modifying your primary
personality style, you will get in the way
of the sale three-quarters of the time.

THE THREE-STEP SYSTEM

You can dramatically increase your selling effectiveness just by using this three-step system:

(a) *Identify the client's primary personality style.* Be observant and try to mentally classify your prospect as one of the four personality styles. Don't carve it in cement, though; people can surprise you. But by "gently" classifying the prospect, you get a "shorthand" set of guidelines in your mind for working with him or her most effectively.

(b) *Suppress the aspects of your primary personality style that are most likely to be most objectionable to the other person.* Depending on your perception of the prospect's style and your understanding of your own, you'll see that there is significant opportunity for friction and conflict in some match-ups. Instead of just charging ahead, consciously control the aspects of your natural, predominant selling style certain to rub the prospect the wrong way.

(c) *Emphasize the aspects of your personality style that are most likely to be most compatible with the other person.* You can also heighten your use of those communication methods likely to be most acceptable to the prospect.

I have two analytical friends and clients, both of whom sell to similar customers. One has very limited success because he never modifies his approach from one customer to the next. The other person does much better. He told me: "My natural tendency is to go into minute, precise detail in response to every question, and for some people that seems right. But I've learned that many customers really suffer when I do that. If you pay attention and have some empathy and sensitivity, you can see their minds fog over, you know they are getting more information than they want. So I work at observing each person's body language, questions, how he or

79

she is dressed, every clue I can get, so that I force myself to abbreviate or elongate my explanations appropriately."

So many salespeople are so busy selling they don't even notice the other person's responses, body language, and facial expressions. These salespeople are human blunt instruments. Instead, if you pay attention and respond as if you were a mirror, so that your body language and speaking style mirrors the prospect's, you'll get much better results.

The bottom line is that modifying your communication style to be more comfortable to the other person makes selling easier and more enjoyable. It relieves tension and increases your closing effectiveness. It is equally valuable in negotiating and even in managing other people.

16

STRATEGY #16:
LONG DISTANCE IS NOWHERE NEAR AS GOOD AS BEING THERE

Some years ago, a company I took over was in deep trouble with a primary, essential vendor. The company owed the vendor a huge sum of money, comprising due and past due bills, some as old as 150 days. The vendor had shut off shipments. They would not even ship COD; they wanted payments on the old bills. The comptroller of our company had tried to work some practical arrangement out with the vendor, and several weeks of correspondence and telephone calls had been invested without any results.

I called the vendor and left word for the president that I was flying in to meet with him, would arrive the following morning, and would stay as long as necessary to resolve the problem in a mutually beneficial manner.

I flew to Minneapolis, rented a car, and drove to the vendor's plant. The president and I met for five hours. I let him vent his frustrations; I let him see that I was not equipped with horns, a tail, and a three-pronged pitchfork and I explained our situation. At the end of the meeting, I had our pending shipments released on an open account, a new open-account credit line sufficient for our needs, and the accumulated amounts due converted to a long-term installment note with no interest. I am absolutely convinced that this could never have been negotiated long distance.

Mark McCormack, arguably the most successful agent-manager of professional athletes today, says: "I will often fly great distances to meet someone face-to-face, even when I can say much of what needs to be said over the phone." I believe this practice is fundamental to his exceptional success at securing and keeping the top athletes and sports personalities as his clients and for negotiating large numbers of lucrative deals for them. He is willing to do what most people are too lazy and too cheap to do: meet face-to-face.

I have negotiated solutions to huge legal disputes, arranged lines of credit under adverse circumstances, raised capital from private and commercial sources, sold large-fee consulting contracts, and otherwise experienced a lengthy list of notable sales and negotiation victories by doing whatever was necessary to get face-to-face with the other person or people involved. In selling a division of one of my companies to a competitor, I didn't bother with preliminary correspondence or a telephone conversation. I just called the company president and said, "I want to fly over and meet with you for an hour or so to present an idea I think you'll be interested in." By starting out face-to-face, I believe I insured the success of the proposition and slashed weeks off the time required to create and close the deal.

There is no substitute for face-to-face, personal contact in selling. Now, I *am* a big believer in substituting tools and other marketing methods for person-to-person contact work in prospecting, as I've described elsewhere in this book. I detest investing productive personal time in meetings with people who are not qualified or ready to do business. But, on the other hand, I very much prefer getting face-to-face with someone who *is* qualified and ready to do business.

Dan Kennedy's Truth About Selling #11
Your financial success will be very closely
related to your ability to minimize your time
spent meeting with people not qualified and
ready to buy, and to maximize your time
spent face to face with people who are
qualified and ready to buy.

PART 2

HOW TO STOP PROSPECTING
ONCE AND FOR ALL

17

POSITIONING, NOT PROSPECTING

It has been my observation that the weakest link in the selling chain for most salespeople is prospecting. Most people can do at least an adequate job of presenting their products or services, if there's a reasonably interested prospect in front of them. But most of the salespeople I've encountered simply hate prospecting. Consequently, they avoid it, both consciously and unconsciously, and do it only when the dire necessity of imminent starvation pushes them to it, and then they do it poorly.

And do you know what? I hate prospecting too. If I had to acquire my clients, my speaking engagements, my consulting assignments, and my writing projects by prospecting, I'd be driving a cab for a living. To me, prospecting is grubby, unpleasant work. To me, there's no worse way to spend time than talking to people who are not interested, are not qualified to say yes even if they were interested, and who view me as someone they have to defend themselves against.

I'm here to tell you: I do NOT think you should prospect.

What you need to do is to focus on positioning. By that I mean *positioning yourself so that good, qualified prospects find out about you and seek you out to obtain your expert assistance in solving their problems.*

Dan Kennedy's Truth About Selling #12
Prospecting sucks.

Why is this so important? Because when you go to prospects and present yourself, their guard goes up. They perceive you as someone there to get something from them. This is when "sales resistance" sets in. But when somebody discovers you, and takes the initiative to seek you out for your expert assistance, then that person's guard is down.

Here are some opportunities for prospects to discover you.

WRITING

Writing and being published is a powerful way of helping others discover you. I've written many articles, for free, for all sorts of publications, and I work hard at having books I've written available in bookstores. Why? Because businesspeople read these articles or books, reach the conclusion that I am the expert who can help them, and then seek me out. If I sought them out and put the same information in front of them, as a sales letter or brochure or even by giving them my books, that would not have a tenth of the impact as when they discover the information for themselves.

How does that apply to you? Let's say you're a car salesperson. You can write an article or a regular column for your community newspaper about the inside secrets of buying, trading in, selling, and financing automobiles. You can write about the tax benefits of buying versus leasing and vice versa, what to look for when buying a used car, how to sell your own car, and so on. If you write a whole series of such articles, there may be newspapers, magazines, "shoppers," local union newsletters, and other publications that would be thrilled to publish them.

You could also write a book. Need ideas? How about *Confessions of a Car Salesperson: How to REALLY Get the Best Deal* or *How to Help Your Teenager Buy and Care for that First Car* or *Everything Women Should Know Before Buying a Car*. Then you could have that book printed and bound and donate a half-dozen copies to every branch library within 100 miles of where you sell cars. Get local bookstores to take them on consignment. Get a busy local car wash to give them away as gifts to their customers. You could even advertise and sell the book by mail.

I have a friend and client, Dr. Robert Kotler, a cosmetic surgeon in Beverly Hills, California, who wrote and published his own book, brilliantly titled *The Consumer's Guide to Cosmetic Surgery*. He has the credibility of an author. The book gets him invited on local talk shows and invited to lecture. He advertises the book rather than directly advertising his practice, and it is one of the best things he's ever done for his business.

If you sell business-to-business, for example, selling advertising time for a radio station, you could write a series of articles about the how-to's of radio advertising and then do everything possible to get them published in local business journals, newsletters, newspapers, and magazines. You could also write and publish a newsletter about the success stories of radio advertising to send out to your clients and selected prospects every month.

PUBLIC SPEAKING

Public speaking is another very effective way to attract favorable attention from people qualified to do business with you. It is also efficient because of the numbers of people reached via each speech.

Open up your local or nearest major city Yellow Pages and look under Associations or Clubs. In Phoenix, where I live, there are over 1,500 listings in this section of the phone book. There are business groups, civic groups, and special interest groups. Most have monthly meetings. Most need speakers. Most don't pay their speakers.

If I'm that car salesperson, and I have a speech: "Confessions of a Car Salesman: How to Get a REALLY Great Deal," I would contact, starting with the As, the Agri-Business Council of Arizona, the American Citizen and Lawmen Association, the American Legion Posts, the American Subcontractors Association, the Arizona Association of Life Underwriters, the Arizona Association of Realtors, and so on. You get the idea.

I'd say to these groups: "Listen, I've got a 30- to 45-minute speech that's fun, funny, and will save your members money the next time they go buy a car."

Even though I get paid to speak, as a professional, I say no to some engagements and yes to others based on how well they position me to be discovered by good, prospective clients. In the last three years, I've appeared in many cities with Zig Ziglar on big, public seminars, with up to 5,000 people in attendance. So why would I travel all the way from Phoenix to Key West, Florida, on a weekend, to speak to 65 people for a lot less immediate income than I get from one of those events with Zig? Because most of those 65 people had paid $7,000 EACH to come to a week-long, intensive seminar to learn how to apply new kinds of direct-marketing methods to their established, existent businesses. They were highly qualified prospects for a number of my professional services. By speaking there, I let them discover me.

Fifteen years ago, when I was just getting started in public speaking, I had limited financial resources for promotion, but I had a lot of time. I did my own telemarketing and spoke for free at in-office sales meetings, real estate offices, insurance offices, and other businesses. In those speeches, I promoted my own seminars. In one year, I did over 150 of these little presentations. I improved my presentations with the practice and I made over $50,000 from promoting my seminars.

Just about anybody could use this same strategy. The founder of the Condom-Mania stores talks about safer sex to college and community groups. A friend of mine who is a computer consultant speaks to any group of business owners he can find, on the subject of "How to Make Money With Your Computer — In Plain English." Actually, you'll be hard-pressed to name anybody in selling who can't use this strategy.

PUBLICITY

Publicity can change your entire life experience as a sales professional. When somebody writes an article about you and it is published in a newspaper or a magazine, or you appear as a guest on a radio or TV show, you gain credibility *and* celebrity.

My friend and client Ryan Elliott is a hypnotherapist. He uses hypnosis in his counseling to help people with phobias and anxieties, depression, binge eating, and other problems. Ryan can advertise but it never does much good because people are naturally skeptical about calling a hypnotherapist. But when they discover him for themselves, that skepticism is replaced by interest. The last time Ryan's local newspaper published an article about him, his practice, and his book, *Wide Awake, Clear-Headed and Refreshed,* he got more than 100 new patients in a matter of days.

The difference in your seeking them versus them seeking you is everything.

ARE YOU JUST ANOTHER SALESPERSON?

You might have the solution to a client's greatest need, the answer to his or her most earnest desire, but if you are perceived as "just another salesperson," the client won't pay attention to you. That's what these techniques are all about: positioning yourself in clients' minds as the expert so that they seek you.

By now you may be wondering how to apply some of these ideas to your own business. *These ideas are transferable, nearly universal strategies that anyone can use.* Suppose, for example, you run a home security systems business.

Easy. Write a book: *Burglars' Seven Secrets for Picking the Houses and Families They Attack.* Write a column for your community newspaper: "Crimestopper Tips." And so on.

You'll find that, just as I said earlier, the writing of a book or a newspaper column will generate business. But you can also use your book to get onto some of the talk shows. Then, watch the news for a new reason why you should appear and be interviewed again, such as a string of robberies occurring in a neighborhood and going unsolved, or the annual release to the media of the crime statistics report.

Next, you could target an appropriate geographic area and start sending a quality newsletter to all the homeowners. Call it *Smart Strategies for Safe Living: How to Safeguard Your Family and Your Home.* Provide useful information and tips. Offer your book free.

You could use your book and newsletter to contact and keep contacting reporters, columnists, and editors of every publication in your area as well as talk show hosts and program directors of radio and TV stations. Be polite but persistent. You'll get written about. You'll get publicity. Then you can quote what they say about you. You might wind up with a selling asset like this: *The Cleveland Plain Dealer* said "Robert Bogart knows more about keeping burglars out than the burglars know about getting in!"

Another publicity idea for your business would be to exploit your success stories. Suppose shortly after you sell and install a security system in the Browns' home, a burglar tries to get in, and is scared away by the alarms. When Ms. Brown calls to thank you with this story, grab your camcorder, get out there, and get her testimonial on videotape. With her permission, you might issue a news release that you can mail to the neighbors.

More ideas: Are you licensed and bonded? Have you been in business for 5, 10, 15 years? How many systems have you installed? How many families sleep safely at night and travel on vacation with peace of mind because you've protected their home and possessions? Have you protected any famous persons' homes? Well-known businesspeople in your area? The credibility and/or celebrity of your customer transfers easily to you.

Now, how do you use all this? Well, let me give you one possible scenario — what I would do in this position. When a call comes in from a homeowner asking me about a security system for his home, I would say: "Mr. Homeowner, I'm extremely busy and cannot do justice to your questions today. However, I have a complete information kit that I'll send to you, and I ask that you review it carefully. Then if you think I'm the right expert to assist you with your home security, call me back. If you choose another source, the information will still help you."

Then I would have a messenger deliver a nice, big box to Mr. Homeowner. Inside the box would be my information kit, which would include —

(a) a copy of my book on home security,

(b) an audiocassette of highlights from my best radio talk show interview,

(c) a couple of copies of my newsletter,

(d) a page of quotes, "What the Media Says About Dan Kennedy, Home Security Expert,"

(e) a page that looks like an article about the Browns', headlined: "Even Though We Thought it Would Never Happen to Us, if We Had Waited Just Three More Days, Our Home Would Have Been Cleaned Out by Burglars!"

(f) a page titled: "All Sources of Security Assistance are NOT Equal," which lists your "credibility items" and statistics, and

(g) a list of famous clients and client testimonials.

Finally, and this is very important, I would include a certificate waiving my usual $250 fee for a home and family protection consultation.

Now, when Mr. Homeowner calls me, what will the positioning be like? Will he perceive me as "just another salesperson?" Not likely.

THE FINAL COMPONENT

Pain, the desire to get relief from pain, physical pain, emotional pain, or financial pain — this is the strongest motivational power of all. From the top-of-the-tower corporate boardroom to the working person's small apartment, people are most moved to stop pain.

I want two things when I'm selling. First, I want someone who knows he or she has a problem that is causing some pain and, second, I want someone who perceives me as the person best qualified and most likely to solve that problem and end that pain.

In the example above of the home security business, I first want the prospective client to call me because he or she feels a need for protection. Then, I want to use "tools," not my time and energy, to let the client arrive at the conclusion that I'm the person best qualified to help take care of that need.

"GEE, THIS SOUNDS LIKE A LOT OF WORK"

Well, I guess it is. But when you compare it to all the work inherent in old-fashioned, traditional prospecting, you'll see that my methods provide a better, continuing pay-off for effort invested.

Salespeople dependent on traditional prospecting have to go to sleep most nights wondering where their next prospect is coming from. They get up most mornings without anybody waiting for them to sell to. These salespeople spend a lot of time hanging around the office, at the coffee shop counter and, in the afternoons, at the movie theater, avoiding prospecting. The sales professional who masters my methods goes to sleep most nights booked solid for the next day with appointments, with people very likely to buy from him or her.

This is more than a choice of business strategies. This is a lifestyle choice.

18

HOW TO USE "LEAD GENERATION ADVERTISING" TO ATTRACT HIGHLY QUALIFIED PROSPECTS

My friend Jeff Paul of Profit Planning Systems teaches certified financial planners, insurance agents and brokers, and accountants how to attract clients with low-cost, targeted, lead generation advertising. His "students" routinely generate 100, 200, even 300 highly qualified leads from only a few hundred dollars worth of advertising. One distributed his lead generation ad via Val-Pak, and got 85 leads for just $300. Another printed his lead generation message on a door-hanger, distributed in a particular neighborhood, got 20 leads, and picked up a $250,000 CD-owner as a client immediately. Another ran his ad in a community newspaper for $122 and got 209 leads! What works for these planners can work for just about any sales professional.

HOW A LEAD GENERATION AD WORKS LIKE A "PERSONALS" AD

If you've ever read, written, or responded to a "personals" ad, you know that they are written to do two things: attract responses from carefully described people and discourage responses from those who do not meet the desired qualifications. The ad might run something like this:

SINGLE WHITE FEMALE seeks single or divorced man, 35 to 49, confident, established in his career, who enjoys travel, theater, cooking, cuddling. No smokers or heavy drinkers, please.

This same approach works for most products or services. You can target your prospect with a lead generation ad. For example, a financial planner might place the following ad:

WARNING FOR MARRIED OWNERS OF BUSINESSES, EXECUTIVES, AND ENTREPRENEURS WITH TAXABLE INCOMES OVER $150,000 PER YEAR:
YOU are the government's #1 target. Your net, combined tax load could as much as DOUBLE in the next 12 months. Your pension fund or retirement savings is at new risk. Do you know the TRUTH about the government's plans for your hard-earned money? MY FREE REPORT: "FINANCIAL ALERT!" reveals the details in plain English (NOT financial gobbledygook) and provides important strategies and tips. If you earn over $150,000, own a business, own your own home, and have a pension or retirement savings plan, this report is for you. CALL: 555-1234.

Clearly this ad "telegraphs" to certain people, and excludes many others, just like a personals ad.

The person who responds to this ad tells the planner several very important things. He or she is married, owns or runs a business, earns over $150,000 a year, owns (or is buying) a home, is saving for retirement, is concerned about taxes, is no fan of the current government administration, and is anxious about his or her finances.

Given all this knowledge about this prospect, the financial planner can create a free report* that directly "hits" this person right where he or she feels it most. The planner then sends the report with the package of promotional materials (see chapter 17, where such a package is described in the example of the security system salesperson).

When the phone rings — and it will — you can be sure that this financial planner is already well-positioned. The

---

* This free report is the equivalent of a sales letter, which is fully described in another book of mine, *The Ultimate Sales Letter* (published by Adams and available in bookstores).

prospective client won't be looking at "just another salesperson" — he or she will be seeking out this planner as the expert most likely to solve personal financial concerns.

WHERE DO YOU RUN
LEAD GENERATION ADVERTISING?

If you sell products or services to businesses, you may use local area business journals and legal newspapers, the business section of your city's daily newspaper, or the trade magazines that serve your clients' type of business. As you probably know, there are national or international trade magazines for virtually every type of business and industry, from aluminum manufacturing to zebra breeding. Also, just about every business has at least one association that publishes and usually offers advertising in a newsletter that goes to its members.

If you need help finding the most appropriate publications to advertise in, visit your public library and consult directories such as *Periodicals in Print* and *Encyclopedia of Associations*.

If you sell products to the general public, you might use your city's daily newspaper, weekly community newspapers, local "shoppers," broadcast media (radio or TV), or coupon packs delivered to residences, like MoneyMailer or Val-Pak.

THE POSTCARD TECHNIQUE

Many salespeople get great results putting their lead generation ad onto a simple postcard and mailing it to lists of likely prospects. The postcard is just about the simplest, least costly advertising vehicle you can find when you consider the cost of a postage stamp.

If you sell to consumers, there are all sorts of mailing lists readily available to you from the very simple, such as all the homeowners in a particular postal region, to something quite complicated, like a "merge-purged" list of subscribers to home decorating magazines who have credit cards, own the homes they live in, and fall into certain age and income ranges, in particular postal regions.

Lists are also available for business buyers including subscribers to certain trade magazines or other publications, compiled lists of business owners or executives by size of business, type of business, annual sales, number of employees, and other criteria.

In most cities, you'll find List Brokers as a heading in the Yellow Pages; one of these local brokers can probably handle simple, local list needs. If you're interested in something more sophisticated, it will pay you to learn a bit about all the lists and list-related services that are available.

Go to the nearest main city public library and ask the business librarian for *Standard Rate and Data Service* (SRDS). Spending an hour or so going through SRDS will open your eyes to a whole world of opportunity! Basically, if you can describe your ideal prospects, you can find available lists to match. And, generally, money spent in list selection is money well spent.

HEADLINES ARE IMPORTANT

Here's a simple "copy secret" for making these postcard mailings work: The headline is the single most important part of the postcard. I find the most powerful headline to be:

> CONGRATULATIONS!
> YOU'VE ALREADY WON:

Then you continue:

> You've been selected to receive a fascinating
> FREE REPORT about
> *your title.*

Then you drop in the rest of your lead generation ad's message. Here's a complete example:

CONGRATULATIONS! YOU'VE ALREADY WON!

You've been selected to receive a copy of automotive expert Bill Gizmo's informative book, *How to Keep Your Car Alive & Kicking at Minimum Cost, Without Ever Getting Burnt by Repair Rip-Offs,* absolutely FREE.

This book is a $9.95 publisher's price value, and it is full of insider information that can save every member of your family money. After all, your family's car(s) represents one of the five biggest investments of your entire life.

Shouldn't you know what insiders — mechanics, race car drivers — know about keeping cars 100% healthy at minimum cost?

Your FREE COPY of this book will be sent to you by mail. There is no cost, no obligation; no strings attached. (This is part of a consumer interest test.) To get your free book, just call (555) 555-1234 and leave your name and address on the recording as instructed.

WHO USES LEAD GENERATION ADVERTISING?

In 1987, a visionary marketer named Jim Bostic switched the entire NordicTrack business from traditional distribution channels to lead generation advertising, followed up by direct-mail and telephone marketing, and the company went from small to giant at a breakneck pace. NordicTrack's ads usually offer a free video to create response.

Many mail-order and catalogue companies use this same marketing model. But not nearly as noticeable, the continent is full of observant, savvy salespeople who have taken note of this model and applied it to their own businesses and careers.

Here are the secrets to making lead generation advertising work for you, too:

(a) Don't try to accomplish too much. The only job of lead generation is to produce leads. Do not try to "presell" your product or service, build business name recognition, or otherwise achieve multiple objectives. Focus 100% on getting the right people to respond. Simply getting the right people to step forward, raise their hands, and identify themselves to you is enough.

(b) Use a powerful, attention-grabbing headline. I've given you a couple of effective examples here. You can come up with others on your own, but remember that the headline must be clear, bold, and simple. It must telegraph the promise of a great benefit. And it's very hard to beat "free" as a component part of what you are offering.

(c) Keep it simple. There's no need to complicate this at all. Focus on a straightforward offer such as a free report, booklet, book, or tape, all of which work very well. Sometimes a free consultation of some kind will work.

(d) TARGET! Write your message to exclude many and attract the relatively few who are perfectly matched with what you have to offer.

(e) A photograph can often improve response to an ad.

(f) Advertising in media read by the people you are trying to flush out is obviously important. You may need to test different media before finding one or two that are consistently productive for you. The necessary experimentation is worthwhile, however, because once you get a lead generation system working for you, it can have a very long life.

Many sales professionals are ultimately able to replace prospecting entirely with lead generation advertising.

PART 3

A NO B.S. START-TO-FINISH
STRUCTURE FOR THE SALE

19
THE SIX STEPS OF THE NO B.S. SALES PROCESS

Last week, my mail contained an invitation to join the American Association of Retired Persons (AARP). It was a beautiful direct-mail package, including a personalized letter, a temporary membership card embossed with my name, and a great premium offer. Only one problem: you have to be 55 to join. It arrived at my place more than a few years too soon. And no matter how great the offer is, I'm not buying.

Many salespeople waste tons of time trying to sell to people who cannot or will not buy. It's not always as clear-cut as in my case with AARP, but it still happens often, for a lot of reasons. Some salespeople are too lazy, too ignorant, or too "chicken" to properly qualify prospects. I know salespeople in business-to-business situations, for example, who know they need to be dealing with the CEO, but insist on selling to the personnel directors, training directors, and sales managers instead. Why? It's easier to get to those people. It takes less confidence and self-esteem to deal with those people. The problem is that dealing with those people is ineffective.

How do you know who is the right prospect?

- Someone who has a reason for interest in your proposition

- Someone with the financial ability to say yes

- Someone with the authority to say yes

- Someone who is predisposed to say yes

Let me quickly explain those four qualifications: first, the prospect has to have a logical reason for interest. Someone who lives in the middle of the Mojave desert is probably a poor prospect for a yacht. A 92-year-old is a poor prospect for life insurance. Those are obvious. The real-life situations you deal with won't be so obvious.

I don't want to encourage you to prejudge prospects to the extreme. However, you need to determine some sensible link between the prospect and the proposition. If you sell furniture, for example, "homeowner" might be the only link needed.

Second, you need someone with the financial ability to say yes. If you sell to businesses, you might want to zero in on companies that have reported growth in the previous quarter (which is a reflection of their financial strength). If you sell swimming pools, aluminum siding, insurance, remodeling, etc., to homeowners, and are going to do a preapproach letter campaign, you might want to have the mailing list of residents in a given area merged with a list of bank credit card holders. The odds are much better that credit card holders are financially able to buy.

Third, you need to talk to someone with the authority to buy. In consumer selling, that often means that both husband and wife have to be present at the meeting. In business-to-business marketing, you have to determine who has the authority to spend how much for what. It is easy to ignore this caveat and be a very busy salesperson who is not very busy selling. In my own selling, I'm usually dealing directly with an entrepreneur who has sought me out — with THE decision-maker.

Fourth, I urge salespeople to concentrate on selling to people predisposed to say yes. In mail-order, for example, we're much better off marketing to known mail-order buyers who also fit our other selection criteria than to people who perfectly fit our selection criteria but have no history of mail-order shopping. If I were selling investment or insurance services, I'd rather contact people who already had some insurance or investments than those who did not. If I sold Lincoln Continentals I would focus on those predisposed to buying big cars: owners of Lincolns, Cadillacs, and Chryslers with cars nearing trade-in age. Beyond that, using the "positioning, not prospecting" strategies presented earlier in this book, you can be sure you are investing your time only with those predisposed to buying — *from you*.

STEP ONE: PERMISSION TO SELL

I believe the first step in the selling process can be best defined as obtaining the prospect's permission to sell. You cannot sell effectively to someone who is mentally or physically backing away from you. Nor can you successfully force someone to pay attention. A person has to choose to be sold to before you can sell to them.

The best device for securing permission to sell is a question structured like this: *If I could show you how to _____ would you be interested in knowing more about it?* Or, if you prefer to be bolder in your assumption, try this: *If I could show you how to _____ you'd be interested in knowing more about it, wouldn't you?*

The prospect who responds positively to this question gives you permission to sell, and you will have actually built a little box around the person, with his or her cooperation, that virtually guarantees subsequently closing the sale. Now all you have to do is fulfill the "if I could show you how to" conditions, point out that you have done so, say "Eureka!" and ask your prospect to "initial right here."

Here is an actual example I scripted for a client of mine in the investment real estate business. When his reps use it, it will work like magic! It is a series of questions:

- Did you pay any federal income tax last year?

- Would you be interested in legally reducing the amount of taxes you pay, providing it didn't cost you anything to do so?

- Could you use $5,000 to $15,000 in extra cash income per year?

- Do you consider yourself an open-minded, positive-thinking person?

- Then, if I could show you how to legally reduce your taxes at no cost to you, increase your income, and associate with others doing the same thing, would you be interested in knowing more?

This series of questions will get the needed permission to sell more than 50% of the time. It can be used in person-to-person prospecting, telemarketing, and advertising.

STEP TWO: THE OFFER

I believe in prefabricating an easy-to-explain, clear, simple, and understandable offer that includes no more than three and preferably only two options.

A two-option offer, commonly called "an either/or" or "an A/B split" usually divides along price lines. You might have a basic, no-frills package at $X, or an options-added, deluxe package at a higher $Y. Another similar approach is to present the deluxe offer, but have a lower cost offer in reserve for a step-down sale.

I'm also a big proponent and user of what I call "the Ginzu knife method" of creating the offer; that is, you offer the main product or service and then add on other benefits. For example, when I offer the Cassette Learning Systems I've been using so successfully for the past several years, I use an A/B split offer. Package A is the basic transfer of my "marketing mind" to yours via the convenience of 18 audiocassettes. I quickly go through the titles of the cassettes, then I show that the regular catalogue price is $139, but at the seminar it's discounted to just $99. Then I use the "Ginzu knife method" by adding a critique certificate worth $100, a copy of one of my books (worth another $10 retail), and a newsletter.

Package B is the same, but adds in my direct marketing action kit, which provides complete, ready-to-use sales letter campaigns, ads, and all other marketing documents for five different types of businesses, plus six more cassettes. I show that this kit alone is catalogue priced at $299, so it and Package A together has a value of $438, plus the bonuses with Package A bringing it up to $548. But for the seminar, I offer everything for just $278. Then I again use the "Ginzu knife method" with a consultation certificate and a double guarantee.

The offer is simply summarized as A, for $99, or B, for $278. It may interest you that I sell at least twice as many Bs as As.

STEP THREE: THE PRESENTATION

There are several "classic" formulas for the structure of a sales presentation. You can find and learn them in a variety of books, tapes, and articles. They have been tested and proven over time. You do not need any new or more sophisticated formulas. You only need to select the one most appropriate to your particular situation.

One formula you'll hear about is AIDA: **A**ttention, **I**nterest, **D**esire, and **A**ction. First, you get the prospect's attention. This is most commonly done by briefly outlining a set of benefits. Next, you build interest by providing evidence of the benefits with facts, statistics, demonstrations, stories, and testimonials. Then, you create desire by relating the benefits to the prospect. You can also build desire with discounts, incentives, or premiums available for prompt action. Finally, you create action with a closing technique.

Another formula is PAS: Problem, Agitate, and Solve. This is the formula I prefer to employ whenever possible. I was using it long before I knew what it was called or that it was, in fact, a known formula.

With this formula, you first state a problem and secure the prospect's agreement that the problem exists. For example, you might agree that there is an epidemic of crabgrass in the neighborhood. Next, you get the prospect agitated about the problem perhaps realizing that crabgrass ruins the appearance of the lawn by damaging the root structure of the healthy grass and that it can damage the lawn mower. Then you produce the solution. Example: Wouldn't it be wonderful if there was a liquid you could spray on your lawn that actually killed crabgrass without damaging the other grass?

This formula is widely used in the advertising of consumer products. The humorous, and memorable, Federal Express commercials do just this.

- The problem: the package didn't arrive.

- Agitation: the employee is in big trouble.

- Solution: "I should have called Federal Express. Why fool around with anybody else?"

I also encourage salespeople to enhance their presentations with visual aids and props. TV has conditioned us to want interesting things to look at. Today, to sell, you almost have to show and tell!

STEP FOUR: EMOTIONAL LOGIC

As far as I know, Zig Ziglar coined the term "emotional logic." It represents the way people buy: they take buying action spurred on by emotional factors, but need logical reasons to justify doing what they really feel like doing.

If you try to get somebody to reason their way to a sale with you, you're going to find tough sledding wherever you go. And I don't care if you're selling sophisticated computer systems to Fortune 500 executives, the act of buying will still occur at an emotional level. If you can't create emotional activity and feelings inside your prospect, you won't make many sales.

But you don't want to be an "emotions steamroller" either. If you do, you'll probably wind up buying back as much as you sell or selling to each customer only once and never building valuable relationships. People require reasons to justify their actions. You need to combine emotion with logic.

The last time I bought a new car, the purchase made a lot of sense because my old car was on the verge of requiring some work, and I had no assurance more repairs weren't going to crop up soon. The same money I was about to spend on repairs could be put into the down payment and, of course, the new car would have a warranty. Also, a new car would be good for my business image and my mental attitude.

Yet, none of those reasons would have motivated me to get the new car if I hadn't *wanted* the new car. You see, a logical argument could be made the other way, too. Even though I needed to put money into repairs for my old car, it was paid off, so there were no payments. Anything less than $500 a month in repairs and I was still ahead of the game in terms of cash flow. The old car looked fine and was perfectly acceptable for my business needs. It was going to take time to shop around and get the new car, and that, for me, represents an expense.

You have heard the saying "Find a need and fill it" all your life as a formula for guaranteed wealth. It is more often a formula for guaranteed bankruptcy. Every week some entrepreneur seeks me out with an invention or a product that really does fill an important need, but cannot be sold success-fully. Why? Because nobody can figure out how to whip up emotional desire for it.

You must merge needs with WANTS. Needs equal logic; wants equal emotion. Most of the time there is a logical argument of comparable strength possible on both sides, for action and against action. And even when there is a legitimate need for the product and a benefit to be gained by having it, that alone cannot tip the scales. The swing factor is emotional.

There are five main emotional factors that motivate peo-ple to action: love, pride, fear, guilt, and greed. Please note, though, that they are all based on a simpler self-interest formula of avoiding pain and obtaining pleasure. For exam-ple, let's say you are soliciting money for a nonprofit organi-zation. Some people might feel guilty about how well off they are compared to the world's poor starving children; they might fear bad luck for not doing their share; they might take pride in being able to help; they might be genuinely inspired by love of humankind; or they might see positive public relations benefits for their business by participating. So all five factors might influence them to participate. But if you go beneath that activity to the very core of response, not giving must be more personally and emotionally painful than giv-ing, and there must be personal and emotional pleasure.

The savvy sales pro tries to push all of these buttons in the presentation.

STEP FIVE: CLOSING THE SALE

I once flew across the country seated next to a grizzled direct-sales veteran who had been a door-to-door vacuum cleaner salesman during the Depression. When hired, he had to study a huge book of answers to 357 different objections and stalls, and learn 357 different ways to close a sale, and take a test on it, before getting out into the field where he could make some money. So he learned all 357. And he told me that in his entire sales career since he'd only used three of them.

I believe that closing the sale should be a natural progression, not some abrupt jack-in-the-box trick you pull out at the end. If closing is difficult, something is wrong with earlier parts of the selling process. You should not have anxiety or stress about the close because it should happen virtually of its own accord, from the momentum you've established. In my own experience, clients will ask: "Okay, how do we get started?" before I even have to "close."

Also, if you've asked a series of trial close questions as you've gone along, you will have established the momentum toward the positive closing and you will have already taken the tension out of asking questions and obtaining answers.

On the other hand, I'm not suggesting you be weak-kneed about closing either. If you aren't fortunate (or good) enough that the prospect jumps ahead of you and literally says "Let's do it," then you need to accelerate your use of assumptions as you approach the close. Salespeople sell their way right out of sales by using "if" instead of "when" terminology. For example, never say "if you become a member," say "when you become a member," or better "as a member, you get...." If you are meeting the prospect in person, match your words with physical action: "Here in your Member Kit, you'll see...."

If you must ask a closing question, there is one simple formula superior to all others. Just about the only closing question structure I bother using or teaching is the simple yes-or-yes question. Would you prefer red or blue? With or without? Today or tomorrow? Pay in three or four installments?

Some people say this is "old hat," and I guess it is. But I haven't found anything better. People usually choose from what's put in front of them. You go into a restaurant, they give you a menu, you choose from the menu. You call up the airline, they tell you what times the flights are, you choose

113

one. So, assuming everything else in the sales process has gone well, a two-option, yes-or-yes question is a comfortable way to close the process.

STEP SIX: THE MORNING AFTER

Here is a secret few salespeople use — not because it is unknown to them, but because they are too lazy to use it. The secret is to insure the satisfaction of the customer after the sale. There are several good reasons to build this step into your sales process.

First, some people suffer from "buyer's remorse." They wake up and feel differently about the purchase a day or two after the sale. The emotion of the moment is gone. They are groping for reasons to justify the action.

Buyers like this need "post-sale reassurance." This can often take the form of a well-written letter that thanks a customer for his or her purchase, congratulates him or her on the purchase choice, and restates the reasons why the decision was such a good one. You might also send or deliver a thank-you or welcome gift, a bonus that was never discussed during the sale.

Second, a customer's first purchase should be the beginning of a long, happy, active relationship. You need to do little things after the sale to cement that relationship.

Finally, if you can create a system that motivates your customers or clients to refer others to you, you will never have problems building a giant income and a secure career in selling. Referrals depend on relationships!

PART 4

MY BIGGEST SECRET TO EXCEPTIONAL RESULTS IN SELLING: TAKEAWAY SELLING

20
THE AWESOME POWER
OF TAKEAWAY SELLING

In this chapter of the book, I reveal *the* secret that I have relied on most heavily in the last handful of years, during which my personal earnings have skyrocketed, along with my prominence in the fields in which I work.

I know that what I share with you in this chapter has the potential to have gigantic impact on your income, and to hold it back seems unfair and selfish. So, here you have it — my personal best technique for exceptional success in selling, what I call Takeaway Selling.

PROVING THE THEORY
OF SUPPLY AND DEMAND

In many ways, Takeaway Selling contradicts classic wisdom about selling. One of the most important underlying principles behind Takeaway Selling is the law of supply and demand and how it affects people's desires. As a rule of thumb, the less accessible something is, the greater the value that gets placed on it and the more people who want it.

I spent too many years of my adult life dead broke, and that was a mystery to me for quite a while. I had my dog-eared copy of *Think and Grow Rich*, kept a car seat full of motivational tapes, went to seminars, faced the mirror and said my positive affirmations out loud every morning, tried hypnosis, subliminals, and every other darned thing, and I had some pretty sharp skills. And I was still walking around with a big, blustery smile on my face with nothing but hungry moths in my wallet. Finally, I determined that the missing link to success is mastering supply and demand because as soon as there is, consistently, a greater demand for your services than there is supply of your time, it's ridiculously easy to be successful.

In my businesses, as a consultant, copywriter, and speaker, I've learned that success definitely breeds success. The busier I am, the more people want my services; the less accessible I am, the more I'm appreciated; the less the supply of me, the greater the demand — and the virtual absence of fee resistance. That's one of the reasons I now publish a frequently updated, detailed copy of my schedule. I send it to clients and prospective clients, and when they see the supply-demand ratio, they act.

These days, this technique is 100% legitimate; I really am overbooked and it is a struggle to fit in new clients, projects, and engagements. But I'll frankly tell you that I did my best to create this appearance and foster this image before it was a total reality. For example, even when I'm in the office, I very, very rarely take an incoming call from anybody but a VIP client, and that's been my policy for years — years before it was a time management necessity. Often to even have a phone conversation with me, it has to be scheduled as an appointment several days to a week in advance.

I also haven't used business cards in years. At speaking engagements, there are always a few people who do not rush to purchase the materials I offer but instead come to me asking for my business card. I tell them that I don't believe in them, and I tell them why: if they aren't interested enough in what I've talked about here to invest a couple of hundred dollars, why would I want them calling me at my office? When new prospects call my office, they're usually advised to send a brief memo to my attention, describing what they wish to discuss with me, so I can then call them at my convenience.

Again, these are now time management necessities. But I implemented them for their sales impact before they became unavoidable.

Dan Kennedy's Truth About Selling #13
When have you ever heard of anybody going to see the wise man at the BOTTOM of the mountain?

A friend of mine sells a high-priced business opportunity. When a prospect answers his ad, he is sent an introductory letter and a four-page questionnaire that must be filled out and returned before my friend will send the company's brochure, other literature, and video tape. Then, before my friend will get on the phone and talk with the prospect, he or she has to complete and send in a second questionnaire and provide three employment or character references. Finally, after their phone conversation, the prospect (called an "applicant" at this point) must get on an airplane, come to the company's headquarters, be interviewed by two different executives, and then, finally, the prospect is allowed to meet my friend and turn in a check and buy the business opportunity.

One of the highest-fee business consultants in America is famous for the fact that he will not get on an airplane — ever. If you want to meet with him, you have got to go to him, and that's all there is to it.

HOW A STARVING DOG TRAINER RID HER FINANCES OF FLEAS, ONCE AND FOR ALL

At a seminar a few years ago, Elizabeth R. cornered me on a break to tell me her troubles. She was a very talented, very capable dog obedience trainer. Her credentials, references, and testimonials were pretty impressive. She had a jazzy brochure. She resided in a high-income area. But she was

119

having a devil of a time making ends meet. "What do you charge?" I asked. "$20 an hour," she answered — and she went to the customers' homes to train their dogs.

I told her, "You are a professional — a dog therapist. Triple your fee, make the client bring the dog to you, and do not even agree to accept a new client's dog until the dog takes your special IQ test for dogs. Charge a fee for the initial client consultation and test the dog to be sure it has enough basic intelligence and the proper attitude to respond to training. And make each new client wait at least a week before you fit him or her in.

"Immediately send a letter to all your past clients, thanking them for all their past referrals but advising them that, because of the overwhelming demand, you have no choice but to impose new restrictions on accepting new clients. Send a similar letter to present clients, but offer them services at your old fees for six more months. Stop answering your own phone. Dress better."

This kind of move takes guts. When you are sitting there, twiddling your thumbs and worrying about the checkbook balance, it requires a lot of nerve *not* to grab that phone yourself on the first ring, jump in, and sell, sell, sell. I know, I've been there.

A few months after the seminar Elizabeth dropped me a note, letting me know she'd had her first $10,000 month, and felt certain she'd make more than $100,000 in the next year.

"CLIENTS SUCK"

For the past few years, Gary Halbert, arguably one of the true geniuses in direct-response advertising, has lived in distant, inaccessible Key West, Florida, where he has hosted advertising seminars that cost $7,000 per person to attend. I have been a guest speaker at every one of them. At the beginning of the first one I went to, Gary arrived in cut-off shorts, a T-shirt, a baseball cap emblazoned with "CLIENTS SUCK!" and an attitude. He quickly told the 60 or so people in the room about several of his horrible experiences with private clients, that he has no desire for any new clients, that, in the rare instances that he accepts one, his fee starts at $15,000, and that he would appreciate it if no one there pestered him during the weekend trying to hire him.

For the rest of the weekend, one attendee after another pursued Gary at every opportunity to sell him on why he should make an exception for him or her.

A REAL ESTATE AGENT TO LEARN FROM

Real estate agent Peggy B. gets 70% of her listings from referrals, 30% from advertising. Either way, when someone interested in listing a home with Peggy calls her office, the receptionist transfers the call to one of Peggy's three assistants. The assistant explains that, because Peggy's services are so much in demand, she employs three client service specialists to, among other things, screen her calls and make certain that the caller's property meets the strict criteria Peggy has for her listings — otherwise the caller will be referred to another agent.

The assistant then asks the caller a dozen questions, completing a form as she goes. Ultimately, an appointment is set for Peggy to visit the client's home several days later.

Next, a videotape "documentary" about Peggy, her unusual success, and the thorough services she provides, is delivered by messenger to the caller's home. The assistant calls the day of the appointment to be certain that both husband and wife have watched the video. In the rare instance where they have not, the assistant postpones or cancels the appointment.

At the appointment time, the assistant, not Peggy, arrives at the home. She bears a gift of a little package of cookies from a local, upscale bakery, and the bad news that Peggy will be delayed by no more than 20 minutes at a closing. In the meantime, the assistant provides information on the recent selling prices of comparable nearby homes, the lengths of times they've been on the market, related data, and how that is used to calculate a reasonable range from which Peggy will determine their best listing price. Peggy tells me it's better to have this "dirty work" done by the assistant before she arrives, giving the client time to think about those numbers versus their all-too-often unrealistic expectations concerning the price.

About fifteen minutes later, Peggy calls from her car phone to announce her imminent arrival. Minutes later, in one of her bright-colored, gold ornament–trimmed Cadillacs, Peggy arrives.

After apologies and pleasantries, she listens as her assistant quickly "briefs" her, summarizing what's been discussed so far and setting up the price range. Next, Peggy asks if, while they talk, it's okay if her assistant goes through the house and takes photographs for potential use in advertising, brochures, and displays at the office. (This, in case you don't recognize it, is a trial close. Why would they let her go ahead with photography if they weren't going to list the house with Peggy?)

The assistant takes her top-quality camera and goes about her business, while Peggy uses her "flip book" to explain the ten steps they'll use together to get the best possible price for the home in the shortest possible time. At the end, there's a listing agreement, already partially completed by the assistant from the information obtained over the phone.

Last year, Peggy listed 92% of the homes where she made this listing presentation immediately, without delay. In almost every one of those cases, Peggy charged an "advertising cost" to the client and collected that from the new client on the spot, too — something most agents do not do. And, of the 8% she did not get immediately, half came to her later.

"What happens," I asked Peggy, "when the client objects to that charge, or the price you want them to set, or they question whether or not you'll be able to give their property's sale enough attention, considering how busy you are?"

She replied: "It rarely happens because of the way our relationship is set up from the beginning. But when it does, I TAKE IT AWAY from them. I'll say something like 'Well, different approaches are right for different people. You may be more comfortable with a more conventional agent, somebody who will sit here day after day on open houses, be around the office whenever you call, and not be so selective about taking clients.' Then I'll pull out my address book and start to recommend a couple of 'those kinds' of agents. The client invariably back pedals."

A FUNDAMENTAL CHOICE

Whether you use Takeaway Selling or not is a fundamental choice about how you are going to go through your career, what kind of experience it is going to be for you and for your customer or clients. Takeaway Selling actually is win-win. Clients feel good about being privileged, being special, being in an elite group, and if they get that feeling by doing business with you, then you are providing significant added value. You will have much more energy and enthusiasm, bring more creativity to your clients' needs, and derive greater satisfaction from your daily experience if you are dealing with people who do feel privileged dealing with you!

PART 5

BONUS UPDATE SECTION

21

THE BRAVE NEW WORLD OF
TECHNO-SELLING

In the last decade, the sales world has been flooded with new technology. There is a plethora of software now available for contact management, time management, automated sending of letters, and so on. There is also, of course, voice mail and its very sophisticated cousins, fax-on-demand and fax broadcasting; e-mail; Internet Web sites; and laptop or even palm-size computers. As you might imagine, I have some "no b.s." observations about all this.

"MR. WATSON, ANSWER THE DARNED PHONE!"

Let's tackle voice mail first. I hate being stuck on the wrong end of this monster, waiting to wade through a menu of choices, pushing "17," and being rerouted to another menu. However, the general public and most businesspeople have become accustomed to using voice mail and, from the sales professional's standpoint, its virtues outweigh its negatives. It's often even better than having a live receptionist or secretary.

The trick to using voice mail as your message taker is to make it as painless as possible for your customers, clients, and prospects. That may mean having one highly publicized number for prospects but another, private number for clients. The voice mail for prospects could have more elaborate and/or different information, screening, and menu options than the number for clients. You do want to manage expectations carefully, though; people leaving voice mail messages will be impatient if not called back quickly, unless you inform them in advance otherwise. If you check messages and return calls frequently all day long, no problem. But if you let an afternoon's messages accumulate until the end of the day and deal with most of them the next morning, your message needs to advise callers of that, to preempt their frustration over your unreturned calls. Also, every sales professional needs a complete strategy for dealing with telephone calls, which I discuss in detail in my book *No B.S. Time Management,* also published by Self-Counsel Press. The telephone can be a huge "time suck" and you need very specific techniques for managing it.

One of the things I like to do with other people's voice mail is to "force" telephone appointments. For example, if I have a dozen or so people who've been trying to reach me, I'll set aside a two-hour block late in the day to call them, virtually certain to get their voice mail, and leave a message that I'll be taking calls at a particular number between x-hour and y-hour the next day. Then I'll say something like: "If you can call me between 9:00 a.m. and 9:30 a.m., that'll be best, but any time between 9:00 a.m. and 12:00 noon is fine. If you get a busy signal, please just call back — do NOT leave a message." Then I'll assign the next couple of people the range of 9:30 a.m. to 10:00 a.m.; the next couple, 10:00 a.m. to 10:30 a.m.; and so on. In about 80% of the cases, I get the return calls exactly when I've asked for them, and I'm able to efficiently handle a long list of calls without playing voice mail phone tag. By the way, you can do this work while sitting out by your pool (or a hotel pool if on the road), enjoying sun and fresh air. You can even take these calls on your cell phone while driving from one city to the next.

The sophisticated options available for voice mail are constantly increasing. One of the companies I use and recommend to my Inner Circle Members* offers a hybrid voice mail service with a live secretarial service. If you wish, your one number in their service can receive voice mail, e-mail, and faxes; translate the e-mail and faxes into spoken-word messages like the voice mail; or transcribe everything and deliver it to you wherever you are by e-mail or fax. You can also call in and dictate responses to go out via e-mail, fax, or a call made for you by one of the secretaries. You can trigger certain callers' numbers to get priority over others and arrange to be tracked down via pager; you can also set up a "find me" process that tries to reach (in the order you request) your office phone, your cell phone, your car phone, your home phone, and your golf cart phone. And you can "reengineer" all that for your convenience day by day, to coordinate with what you'll be doing and where you'll be that day. It's really quite remarkable.

LET THE PHONE DO SALES WORK FOR YOU

A variation of regular voice mail is the "recorded message" that dispenses information automatically so you don't have to. This goes beyond message-taking into automated information delivery. For example, many real estate agents now build a menu into their voice mail so prospects calling for information about currently listed and available properties can press 1 to hear about west side properties, 2 for lake side, or 3 for downtown condos. In fact, the #1 agent in the entire RE/MAX organization year after year, a client of mine, Craig Proctor of Toronto, pioneered the use of this technology in selling real estate and now teaches an entire marketing system built around it to other agents. At last count, he had well over 3,000 real estate agents all over North America following his model and selling more with less work.

---

* We publish a resource directory for our Inner Circle Members, and maintain a resources section on our Web site. For more information, go to <www.inner-circle.com>, or you can request information by fax: (602) 269-3113.

The advertised "free recorded message" often boosts response to advertisements, sales letters, brochures, or catalogues, and is an effective and efficient prospecting tool for sales pros — just as it is an advertising tool for business owners. For example, my friend and client Rory Fatt, of Restaurant Marketing Systems in Vancouver, Canada, teaches restaurant owners how to use the free recorded message as a means of running smaller, cheaper ads and then dispensing information about the restaurant, cuisine, chef's expertise, specials, events, and opening hours via a recorded message. Another long-time client of mine, Jeff Paul of Profit Planning Systems in Chicago, teaches financial planners and insurance agents how to prescreen and qualify prospective clients by filtering them through an informative recorded message.

JUST THE FAX, MA'AM

Remember that guy in *Dragnet* always saying, "Just the facts, ma'am?" Maybe I'm dating myself. And by some people's standards, the fax machine is dated too. I, however, am still in love with the fax machine and all that it can do to facilitate the selling process. (It's my kind of technology: one button.) First, it lets you respond quickly (if not instantaneously, at least without mail delay), easily, and at virtually no cost to requests for information and quotes. Since the fax accurately reproduces what you send (unlike e-mail, to be discussed later in this chapter), you can transmit sales letters with all the embellishments (such as underlining and boldface type) and be assured it will reappear at the other end as intended.

One of the best benefits of communicating by fax is that, in most offices, incoming faxes still get priority over incoming mail. Your fax leaps to the top of the pile. In many businesses faxes are treated like phone messages, in that they are dispensed to or picked up by recipients a number of times each day, instead of being in one fat daily stack of mail.

It's also easier to get past "gatekeepers" to decision-makers (if you know their name) with a fax than with mail. The combination of a fax's immediacy and perceived priority, use of a personalized cover sheet, and separation from mail routinely screened and sorted by the gatekeeper often guarantees the fax safe passage to the decision-maker's hands.

There simply is no other medium that combines this kind of favored priority handling with its near-zero cost.

One of the most interesting uses of the fax for prospecting purposes is "broadcast fax." This tool is very useful in situations where you are seeking qualified leads from a large pool of potential prospects. For example, a client of mine, Michael Kimble of Group M Marketing in Austin, Texas, sells training and business courses in several niche markets: to print shop owners, travel agency owners, and doctors. In each of these groups, he is able to use broadcast fax to mass-fax a simple one- to two-page lead generation letter offering free information, and typically get a 5% to 10% response. It's all done by a service bureau at a very nominal cost, with all the delivery instantaneous and simultaneous — so he gets most results within a couple of days. This kind of marketing is much more immediate than any other affordable approach. It beats cold-calling on the phone, for example, by a long shot.

Although Michael completes all his sales long-distance, this is perfectly applicable to any sales professional seeking appointments with corporate executives, business owners, or doctors. The process is as follows:

(a) Create a one- to two-page fax with a compelling head-line, offering free information (e.g., a free report, booklet, or tape) of clear relevance to the prospect, which he or she can request by faxing back a form or business card.

(b) That information is then sent or delivered, along with a sales letter that sells the appointment (e.g., free consultation or free review). Some prospects will call you themselves to schedule an appointment. You can make follow-up calls to those that don't.

A client of mine, Hal Mohan, an investment adviser, uses this strategy in Cincinnati to secure appointments with business decision-makers. He has his two-page initial letter offering a free report faxed to 1,000 CEOs and business owners on the first day of each month. Twenty-five to as many as 100 people respond and request the report. The report convinces them to meet with Hal, and most months he secures 5 to 15 appointments with good prospects. Of those, about half immediately sign on as clients. Hal *never* makes cold prospecting calls. In fact, he never talks to someone until they have qualified themselves by responding to the fax and asking for the information, presold themselves on Hal and his expertise by reading the report, and then proactively called him to ask for a meeting.

In my work as a consultant helping sales organizations devise effective, integrated marketing-prospecting-selling systems, and then teaching their salesforces how to use them, the "Hal model" I just described is the one I use most frequently.

This model can also be especially valuable to traveling salespeople or territory representatives. They can send a broadcast fax to all their accounts and prospects in the city they'll be working in a few days down the road, alerting them that they'll be coming by and arousing curiosity about a new product, demonstration, or opportunity. Upon arrival, they'll easily be able to get appointments with prospects in person.

One other smart use of the fax is having a fax-on-demand system. This system can be especially useful if you sell a variety of different products or your product has a lot of technical data, specifications, or accumulated related articles and research. This information can be set up as documents, that are stored and made available for automated, instant faxing to anyone who dials in, enters the "stock number" of the documents desired, and enters his or her fax number. I know one sales professional in a very technical field who has about 100 different documents listed in his ads and on a little card he gives to all his prospects and clients. Prospects can telephonically request and instantly receive by fax any number of these documents without any manual labor on his or his staff's part.

LAPTOP SELLING

These days, many sales representatives are reducing the number of samples, audiovisual equipment, or demonstration tools they schlepp around with them, and are creating dynamic sales presentations thanks to their laptop or notebook portable computer. Graphs and charts formerly presented flat in flip books can now be rendered in three dimensions on the computer screen. Testimonials can come to life with photos or even full-motion video and sound. The workings of products like industrial equipment can be demonstrated on the computer. And presentations can quickly and easily be personalized for each prospect in advance or by plugging in information and making calculations during the presentation. All this pretty much antiquates flip books, flip charts, portable video players, and, of course, legal pads.

A caution, though: As a professional speaker, I've watched similar technology invade our business. Presentations have gone high tech, with full-color computer graphics, multiple-screen presentations, and laser pointers replacing overhead transparencies. When a truly accomplished and effective speaker chooses to use these tools to enhance a presentation, the results are sometimes very impressive. But there are two risks: One, the mediocre or unprepared speaker may use these tools as crutches to disguise a poor presentation. Tools doth not a carpenter make. Two, the gizmos and techno-effects can be so dazzling they distract from the message. I've seen both risks realized many times. My belief is that a true pro can walk out onto a plain stage with nothing but his mind, mouth, and body and hold an audience spellbound and effectively communicate, persuade, and motivate without need of electronics. And most of the highest-paid, most-in-demand, and best-known speakers in the country — like my speaking colleagues Zig Ziglar, Jim Rohn, Tom Hopkins, and Brian Tracy — do just that.

Similarly, I think a true sales pro can command the attention, stimulate the interest, and secure the conviction of his prospect on the strength of his knowledge, "pitch," and enthusiasm — without reliance on special effects. If you need these things to function, then you are not functioning as well as you could and should be.

So, my "rules" are —

(a) use these techno-wiz sales tools sparingly;

(b) use them for good reason, not just because they're available or because you think they're "cool"; and

(c) do not lazily rely on them to compensate for lack of knowledge, preparation, or selling skill.

One of the most popular training programs about using the laptop computer as a sales presentation tool is called Shoulder to Shoulder Selling, and you can get information about it at <www.teamdenver.com>.

CAUGHT UP IN THE WEB

North America has been turned on by the Internet. It's my observation that many salespeople, even entire sales organizations, have become so caught up in it, they are wasting tons of time on the Internet that should be invested in selling. The Internet is seductive technology and, at the moment, still a vastly over-hyped opportunity. However, there are a few legitimately useful Internet applications for sales pros.

The first application is *e-mail*. Its virtues are that it's fast, virtually instant, and virtually free. If a significant percentage of your clientele is online, they will want to be able to communicate with you by e-mail, and you will probably want to accommodate them. People are using e-mail as a faster, cheaper, easier replacement for the fax machine and fax-on-demand. You can set up "auto responders" that e-mail literature, sales letters, or other information back to your prospects and customers on request without you or any other person having to lift a finger.

One caution about e-mail, however: direct-mail pros like me are still disturbed by the lack of control we as senders have over the look of the information when it is received. When you use print letters to prospect or to sell, cosmetic tricks like underlining, boldfacing, varying the size of the type, varying the typestyles, and adding handwritten margin notes are nearly as important as the copy itself. However, some of these tricks you can't (yet) do with e-mail, and others you can do but can't guarantee they won't be undone by the recipient's computer or printer. Simply put, you sacrifice a lot for the sake of speed and convenience of e-mail. With that in mind, it's my contention that e-mail is better used for routine correspondence than for sales correspondence, and better used for disseminating technical information than for selling. This is changing, and it probably won't be long before I modify my position.

The second sales application of the Internet is a *Web site*. The costs of putting together and maintaining your own Web site keep dropping. What started out costing tens of thousands of dollars is down in some cases to under a thousand dollars for a well-designed, up and running Web site — and I mean designed by somebody who not only understands the technology but also understands sales and marketing. There's even off-the-shelf software you can use to do it all yourself if you're so inclined. (But watch the time trade-off. Know what your hours are worth if out there selling instead of sitting in front of the computer!) For more information on creating a Web site, take a look at Self-Counsel's *Winning Web Sites.*

Can you sell via a Web site? Actually, yes. One of my clients and a member of my Platinum Inner Circle, Barry Shamis, recently gave our whole Platinum Group a demonstration of how he simulates a face-to-face sales presentation using his Web site. Barry sells and provides high-priced training programs to corporate executives on the subject of "selecting winners": finding, interviewing, choosing, and hiring the right employees. A single training contract may run between $15,000 and $150,000. And often, Barry has to attend a face-to-face meeting to secure the contracts. Increasingly though, he is talking with the prospective client on the phone, asking if they're online, and, if they are, having them pop up his Web site in front of them while they are speaking on the phone. Barry then talks the prospective client through the Web site over the phone, somewhat like a salesperson might use a flip chart or flip book if sitting across the desk from the prospect. He is closing sales this way, without leaving his office.

A more common use of the Web site by salespeople is as an alternate means of delivering sales literature. One of my Inner Circle members, Bryan Dean Toder, a professional magician who works with many corporate clients, explains that when prospects call his office and ask to have information sent to them, he or his staff always asks if they have access to the Internet. If they do, they're directed to his Web site at <www.wizardmarketing.com>, where all his literature is posted and instantly available. By making everything instantly available, he says he beats out competition who respond by mail with days of delay.

If you sell in a highly competitive environment, such as insurance or financial services, where there is little difference between products and claims that can be made for the products, having your own Web site that is well-stocked with accessible, useful information, including articles and reports you've written, can help set you apart from the crowd as an expert and as someone on the cutting edge of your industry.

The most important thing to keep in mind about your Web site is that it will rarely scoop up and deliver good prospects to you on its own. Instead, it is one more literature-type tool that you can use when you choose to direct your prospects or customers to it.

TOOLS AND TOYS

The fellow that sat down next to me on an airplane the other day had his laptop; a modem to connect it to the air phone; his cell phone; a pocket-sized computerized name, address, and phone directory; and a text-message beeper. This guy was so wired up and wired in he couldn't get loose to go use the bathroom! His disdain for me, sitting there writing notes on three-by-five-inch cards, was palpable. We were destined never to become golfing buddies. Besides, he'd need a U-Haul trailer behind the golf cart just to lug around all his gadgets. Unless you're a heart surgeon, I do not believe you need to be that connected. And for many salespeople, it's actually better not to be so readily accessible (reread chapter 20 of this book about Takeaway Selling).

I also played a game with another business traveler a few weeks ago: against the clock, we each had to find five phone numbers of clients or important contacts; he from his whiz-bang computerized doohickey, me from my stapled together yellow pages of names and numbers. I won.

If something is legitimately a useful, time-saving, productivity-enhancing tool for you, then I'm all for it. But sometimes it's hard to tell tool from toy. Don't get caught up in a contest to carry around more gadgets than the next person.

CONTACT MANAGEMENT TOOLS

I'm a big believer in staying in constant and frequent communication with clients, targeted prospects, and other important contacts. And if automating that process helps you to do it, I'm all for that — as long as you don't sacrifice the personal touch. For example, you can have your computer kick out e-mails or even regular letters to a list of clients every x-number of days. But none of that will ever substitute for you having clipped an article from a magazine about fly fishing, jotted a handwritten note, and sent them to a client who is passionately interested in fly fishing.

There's plenty of off-the-shelf software in the contact management category that can cater to your needs. There are also specialists in this field who design and provide generic and customized contact management systems for sales professionals. Most of them routinely advertise in *Selling Power Magazine*, which every sales professional ought to be reading (check out <sellingpower.com>). At the 1998 Salesforce Automation Software Trade Show in Chicago, there were 140 different vendors displaying various kinds of sales automation software, so this is a growing field, both in size and sophistication.

STILL CAN'T BEAT IN-THE-FLESH SELLING

Admittedly, I am — by conditioning, preference, and age — a low-tech person in a high-tech world. This makes me cautious. For example, there are credible studies cropping up indicating that people who spend even a few hours a week on the Internet are more subject to depression than those who don't, and that people using the Internet for several hours every day are very subject to depression. Researchers theorize this has to do with the isolation of the medium. For me, this validates my own anxiety about stripping human relationships out of the process of doing business. I worry about the sales professionals who are so into automation that they actually achieve isolation.

There's a TV commercial where a company president calls his staff together, tells them they're losing customers, and that one they lost told him: "You just don't seem to care about us anymore." The president then starts handing out airline tickets, telling everybody they are getting out of the office, into the field, and visiting all their accounts in person again — much to the groans and consternation of the troops. It's not a very good commercial because I can't for the life of me recall what it's selling; maybe an airline or a hotel chain. But I thought the scenario itself was profound.

The late Cavett Robert, founder of the National Speakers Association and one of the best salespeople I've ever known, was famous for his line: "They don't care how much you know until they know how much you care." Yep, it's trite. But it is NOT antiquated.

Prospects, customers, and clients at all levels, from the kitchen table to the corporate boardroom, still buy on emotion and justify with logic. They still must have an emotional, personal connection with a salesperson; they will not buy sophisticated or expensive goods and services from a vending machine. This should make you cautious about putting too much distance between yourself and your customer via technology.

AFTERWORD

I hope you enjoyed reading this book. If you would like a free copy of my book *How to Solve All Your Advertising, Marketing, and Sales Problems,* a catalogue of my other books, cassettes, seminars, and services, and information about my "No B.S. Marketing Letter," please contact me.

Dan Kennedy
5818 N. 7th Street, Suite #103
Phoenix, Arizona 85014
Fax: (602) 269-3113

OTHER DAN KENNEDY TITLES AVAILABLE FROM SELF-COUNSEL PRESS

If you have enjoyed this book, you're sure to want to read Dan Kennedy's other titles.

- *No B.S. Business Success*

- *No B.S. Time Management*

If you would like to receive a free catalogue of all Self-Counsel titles, please write to the appropriate address below:

Self-Counsel Press	Self-Counsel Press
1704 N. State Street	1481 Charlotte Road
Bellingham, WA 98225	North Vancouver, BC V7J 1H1
USA	Canada

141

BONUS CHAPTER FROM
NO B.S. SALES SUCCESS

HOW DO YOU KNOW
IF YOU HAVE A REALLY GOOD IDEA?

This bonus chapter is taken from Dan Kennedy's book *No B.S. Business Success,* **also published by Self-Counsel Press.**

Wilson Harrell, entrepreneur and business consultant, has a unique way of testing a new product, service, or business idea. He calls it the "Well, I'll be damned!" test. Harrell suggests taking a sample of your idea to at least 20 potential buyers (not friends, relatives, or neighbors!) to see how they react. If they don't say, "Well, I'll be damned" or "Why didn't I think of that?" you do *not* have a winner.

If most of the people do say the magic words, ask them other questions, such as: What would you be willing to pay for this? If it were available at that price, would you definitely buy it? Maybe buy it? Why? How would you use it? Do you think it's such a good idea you might want to invest in it? Why? Why not?

This brings us to the most important rule of entrepreneurial marketing I can think of.

Dan Kennedy's Eternal Truth #4
You cannot trust your own judgment.
Test, test, test. Then test some more.

Are entrepreneurs impatient by nature? Maybe so, but successful entrepreneurs must learn to be patient sometimes.

Testing is one of those times. Anytime you can, anyway you can, test.

ASK YOUR CUSTOMERS

At Stew Leonard's famous store, management regularly meets with groups of customers over coffee and doughnuts to ask them what they like, what they don't like, what they'd like done differently, what they think of a new product or service.

A major electronics and appliance retailer took the trouble of finding out what his stores' customers liked best and least about buying televisions, stereos, and appliances. One comment was so frequent and consistent it stood out like the proverbial sore thumb: people hated having to block a whole day out of their schedules and wait around for the delivery of what they purchased. He developed a system to provide instant delivery with purchase or scheduled delivery, with the delivery time guaranteed within a two-hour range. This service became his main advertising promise — with fantastic results!

ASK YOUR COUNTERPARTS AND COMPETITORS

One of the easiest, quickest research tasks every business owner must do is to go to the library, get the Yellow Pages directories from other major cities, and look through all the advertising in your category of business. You will inevitably find advertisers somewhere doing something nobody in your area is doing, and that should give you some good new ideas. As well, you may also find somebody offering a product or service that you have considered. It won't hurt to call them and talk to them about their experiences. You might even go visit them.

The same holds true for your competitors. You probably can't have a direct talk with them, but you can check up on them. I'm amazed at the businesspeople who never go to their competitors' stores or buy their products. Michelle Comeau, a customer service consultant based in Las Vegas, conducts "incoming call handling audits" for her clients; she'll call all a client's competitors, pretend to be a prospective customer, and ask a lot of questions. From the answers, she can detect areas of opportunity.

DIRECT MAIL

One of my earlier books, *The Ultimate Sales Letter,* is all about how to create good direct-mail campaigns and sales letters, even if you know nothing about writing. I wrote that book because I believe direct mail is the very best way most entrepreneurs have available for marketing their products and services for the simple reason that it is the easiest to test results.

Other types of advertising are much more difficult to test. How do you test a Yellow Pages ad, for example? That same ad is stuck there for 12 months; you can't change it. The most frustrating thing about producing TV infomercials — something I do a lot — is the inability to test different ideas, promises, and offers without actually putting together a show at great expense.

Direct mail offers the unique opportunity to do cheap testing. You can tell a lot from tests as small as a few hundred pieces mailed, depending on the market, lists used, and other factors. This means you can "split-test" one letter against another or one offer, price, or premium against another, for just a few hundred dollars. And, once you find a campaign that works, you can keep on testing other variables cheaply and easily, to try to make it better. Best of all, once you find that success formula, you will probably be able to use it to get consistent, successful results for years.

USE ALREADY-TESTED
DIRECT MARKETING CONCEPTS

But what if you can't test? First of all, you need to know as much as you can about what works and what doesn't in your particular business. You need to do your homework on your industry, your counterparts, your competitors, and your customers. Simply, the more you know, the better your "guess."

Let me tell you a secret. I get paid a great deal of money to "create" brilliant marketing ideas, but I doubt that I've ever honestly done that. Inventing a new idea is a lot of work. Stealing a successful idea is a lot faster, easier, and more likely to yield successful results. So, I try to "steal" whenever I can.

For example, I was recently hired to write a full-page magazine ad for a money-making opportunity, so I needed a "killer" headline. I found the two most successful ads I had seen for other money-making opportunities, took the best parts from each, and combined them into a new headline. Then I changed the details to match my client's offer. This ad is working like gangbusters. The headline creation process took me 20 minutes. To have thought it up from scratch could have taken 20 hours.

A friend with a specialty retail store came to me in need of an idea to stimulate a fast surge of cash flow. Fortunately, he had a mailing list of his past customers, so he could get the job done with a great sales letter. I pulled a letter out of my files, one a chiropractor had used to promote a "patient appreciation" event, and said, "Here, sit down and rewrite this letter. Don't change much except the details for your products." It took him only one hour to compose a letter that brought in over $30,000 in 15 days.

Given the right resources, you can go a long way on 100% borrowed, already-proven strategies.

MOVING IDEAS FROM ONE BUSINESS
TO ANOTHER

To the best of my knowledge, the drive-up service window belonged to the banking industry before anybody else latched on to it. But it sure does account for a lot of the fast-food industry's sales. It's also used by dry cleaners, video rental stores, and florists. There are probably others using it that I haven't noticed and still others who could and should be using it.

Somebody in the fast-food business "stole" this idea. My vision is of a McDonald's executive sitting in his car in the bank drive-in line on Friday afternoon when it hits him — Hey, I don't think we can fit the milkshakes in the little tube, but outside of that, this could work for us!

Just about every idea came from something already created or used. The very successful "Amazing Discoveries" format for TV infomercials is a cross between a game show and a state fair barker demonstrating the magic slicer-dicer to a gathered crowd. Club Med is a cruise ship set up on land. *Star Wars* is an updated version of the classic Western movie.

HOW TO BE MORE CREATIVE

Most entrepreneurial fortunes are made without brand new ideas. Instead, entrepreneurs tend to alter, combine, and "twist" proven winners. Here are a few of the creativity formulas for getting this done. Look for these or other principles behind everything you encounter. Pretty soon this will be a habit of thinking, and you'll automatically be more creative!

(a) *If you can't change the product, change the package.* Cheeseburgers. With bacon, without bacon. Round, square. Now what? After just about everything that could be done to a cheeseburger had been done to a cheeseburger, McDonald's created the McD-L-T. Remember? Keeps the hot side hot, the cold side, cold. The product stayed the same; the package changed.

(b) *Make it bigger.* Big screen TVs, "home theaters." Gilleys, THE largest country-western night club in America. 7-11's Big Gulp.

(c) *Make it smaller.* How about a TV that fits in your pocket? One-serving sizes of pudding, yogurt, microwaveable spaghetti.

(d) *Add to it.* Shampoo plus conditioner in one. Cold capsules enriched with vitamin C. A bookstore-café combination.

(e) *Subtract from it.* The convertible (a top-*less* car). Foods with no preservatives. No Appointment Hair Cutters, a successful national no-frills chain of salons.

(f) *Do it faster.* The ten-minute oil change. Speed-dialers for telephones. The microwave oven — once thought only saleable to restaurants, by the way.

(g) *Do it slower.* The car wash by hand.

(h) *Do it cheaper.* Cubic zirconia jewelry. K-Mart.

(i) *Do it more expensively.* The Nieman-Marcus Christmas catalog, filled with very pricey, unique gifts, gets millions of dollars of free publicity every year. First-class air travel.

WHAT IF EVERYBODY HATES YOUR IDEA?

A lot of very smart people did nothing but discourage Walt Disney. A lot of very smart people told Dave Thomas the fast-food hamburger business was saturated. I'm sure we could fill a whole shelf full of books with similar examples. There's probably a product in every room of the house that was once criticized as a dumb idea.

148

If you really have faith in your idea, even if no one else does, and you go in with your eyes open knowing you may lose, then — charge! On the other hand, keep in mind that the true entrepreneur marries goals and objectives, not isolated ideas. When one of your ideas does prove itself unprofitable, don't try to raise the dead; move on to the next method of achieving your goals.

In 1941, 8th-grade dropout and bakery delivery man Carl Karcher mortgaged his car for $350 to buy a hot dog stand. His first day's sales were an unexciting $14.75. But, by 1946, more hot dog stands followed, and then hamburgers and "Carl's special sauce" were added. Today, the Carl's Jr. chain includes more than 400 restaurants, all based on serving a top-quality hamburger. The unique factor is what Carl calls "partial hostess service." His are the only fast-food joints where you place your order, sit down with your beverages, and wait for an employee to bring your fresh-cooked food to you, rather than standing around waiting at the counter.

But around 1983, Carl had a bright idea that didn't work out. Like all fast-food places, the bulk of the business was breakfast and lunch. Carl decided to buck that norm and go after the family dinner business. He introduced new char-broiled dinner platters — steak, chicken and fish — at all the restaurants, and invested heavily in advertising and promoting these new items to woo customers in at dinner hour. Even the signs on all the locations were changed from Carl's Jr. Charbroiled Hamburgers to Carl's Jr. Restaurant. Millions of dollars were poured into this new approach.

Instead of adding revenue, the dinner idea confused franchisees, managers, and the public. Average annual sales per location dropped. In 1985, Carl Karcher had to face up to the fact that his Big Idea was a flop. He dug in and started leading his company back to its reliable roots. The signs were changed back, menus simplified, prices cut, and the advertising spotlight returned to the famous charbroiled hamburgers. Sales almost immediately started climbing.

In January 1988, Carl Karcher told *Nation's Business Magazine*, "The stress these last several years has probably been greater than at any time in my life. When you've put in 45 years, you think that everything's going to get easier. Nothing is easy! And I think that's where too many people fail in business — they think they've got it made. It's fun being in business, but there's no risk for the wicked."

Carl Karcher's certainly had many good business ideas during his career, and he has backed those ideas with his faith and with action. But, as his story shows, nobody gets by without having a clinker now and again. You will too. So, go ahead, have the guts to act on those you really believe in — and the good sense to walk away from those that prove unrewarding.